T0208693

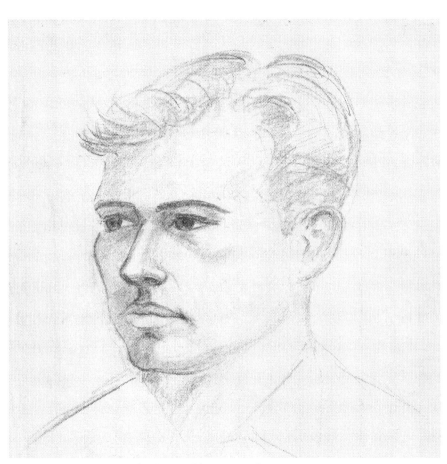
Authors self-portrait. Circa 1960.

# A Modern Fairey Story

Derek Fairey

**author**HOUSE®

*AuthorHouse™ UK*
*1663 Liberty Drive*
*Bloomington, IN 47403 USA*
*www.authorhouse.co.uk*
*Phone: UK TFN: 0800 0148641 (Toll Free inside the UK)*
*        UK Local: (02) 0369 56322 (+44 20 3695 6322 from outside the UK)*

*Published by AuthorHouse 11/02/2023*

*ISBN: 979-8-8230-8460-4 (sc)*
*ISBN: 979-8-8230-8461-1 (hc)*
*ISBN: 979-8-8230-8459-8 (e)*

*Library of Congress Control Number: 2023917125*

*Print information available on the last page.*

# Contents

# Forward

As a very young child, I learnt what I call, the rudiments, of dealing with any stress that may occur in my life. The occurrence that happened is still a very clear picture in my head and was confirmed by both my mother and my aunt Lil, separately, later in my life. It was during the second world war and I had just learnt to walk and talk, only just.

Another of my aunts was Dorothy, who was, at twenty-four years of age, very pretty but suffering from cancer, which was about to cause her death, at any moment.

The video which plays out in my head, even eighty years later, is still very sharp and clear and is as follows:-

I am a very small child, sitting behind a dining chair which has what is called an 'H' bar between the legs, to strengthen them, that is fact from the time and knowledge, picked up in later life.

I look between the legs of the chair, and I can see the window with a single bed stretched under it along the wall beside it. There are three people sitting on the bed, my aunt Lil, on the left, my mother on the right, and in the middle is aunt Dorothy, crying. The two either side of aunt Dorothy are trying to comfort her and I, seeing someone obviously upset, am curious and feel I want to be with them. Being a child, I do not go round the chair, I crawl through underneath and directly towards them.

When I reach them, I pull myself up on the stockings aunt Dorothy is wearing. She looks at me, with her tear filled eyes and I make the comment which is most relevant, without realizing it.

I say, "Don't cry aunty Dothry, suck a sausage." They three all react with small laughs, aunty Dorothy's laugh, choked out more than anything, but I get a cuddle and am sent lovingly on my way.

Later in life, when I am reminded of the incident, both by my aunt Lil and my mother at different times, cementing it in my memory, I realize, I had learnt something, subconsciously and without realizing it. This probably combined with the reactions I witnessed of people, naturally reacting badly on hearing bombs exploding almost on top of them.

When a stressful situation occurs, I automatically become calm and carry on. My mind then allows me to react very efficiently and come out the other side in the best condition.

This helps to explain how I have survived many of the situations in my life, I write about and why my descriptions, sometimes appear very, matter of fact.

When I read things back, I get the impression that I have somehow removed a lot of the emotion that was there at the time. I must apologize for this, done in the interest of brevity, because so many scenarios exist in my life story and I ask you to read on and not get bored or start misbelieving the truth of it all.

In places, in the book, I have repeated previous wording. Forgive me if this becomes boring. One reason for this is the many troubles I have had with hacking and computer glitches that have occurred. This is not so much a fault, it is a lead in to a different story which is related in some way.

# A Modern Fairey Tale

At approximately 7.00am on the second day of January 1909 Mrs Mary Lane (nee Drake) gave birth to a bouncing baby daughter. Mary's forebears had once been able to claim a somewhat higher station in life. Unfortunately life and it's vagaries had altered that and here was Mary giving birth to her daughter in The London Hospital which catered for the local 'cockney' and other London 'east enders'. The local population spoke in a chirpy type of way and their interest in words had given rise to what is known as 'Cockney Rhyming Slang'.

Ten minutes later Mrs Fairey, a true cockney of the working class, gave birth to a baby boy in the same hospital. It is not known whether the two Mothers knew each other or not. It is known however that some years later their two offspring met, fell in love and married. So Florence Mary Lane became Florence Mary Fairey, Wife of Arthur Richard Fairey. This in spite of some reservations on the part of Mary Lane, her Mother. After all the Lane family tended to pronounce their words a little better and show a little bit more intellect in general.

Arthur proved to be a very loving Husband who did his very best to give his wife and four children the best he could in life. He had started his working life at the age of thirteen years of age, approximately, in a rope making business in the docks area of London. His ambition and general attitude however earned him the opportunity to become a 'Ship Fitters Mate' in the actual docks.

As children, of course, Arthur and Florence had lived through the First World War. They had a son James Arthur, born on 12th September 1934 and a second son Arthur Charles born on 5th April 1938. On the declaration of what was to become The Second World War starting in

September 1939, they feared that they would be parted when Arthur would inevitably be called to fight for his country. They got together to comfort each other and their third and last son, Derek Richard was conceived and was born on 2nd July 1940. They were determined however to have a daughter and Jean Mary was born on 24th January 1944.

This is the story of the life of Derek the youngest son of the family. Born when his brother Arthur was only two years and three months old this meant that when his Mother was attending to Arthur someone needed to look after him. This job most often used to fall to his Aunt Lillian, the younger Sister of his mother, thus the first interesting story about Derek was as follows.

Having been made homeless by Hitler's bombs, like many people in the east end of London, the Fairey family, through the good offices of a friend of Florence, found one room in a house, where the friend also lived, in Spencer road. However a few days before Derek was born the friend was so upset by the conditions of life that she put her head in the gas oven to try to commit suicide. This obviously upset Florence and she was advised to move out, if she could, to temporary accommodation until the child (Derek to be) was born.

The only place where she could go at the time was her Father in Law's flat. Her Father in law was the foreman of a Cartage company which used only horses and carts at that time. He lived in a flat over the stable and should have got special permission from his boss. He did not get this permission but Florence moved in regardless and a few days later, on the second of July Derek was born.

This meant that Derek was born in a stable while his mother and father were in temporary accommodation there. The war conditions meant that there were bright lights (searchlights) in the sky at the time but there the similarity to another 'well known' historical character ended. Other than the fact that they were both male. However, to protect his Grandfather, the birth was not registered at that address, and because the single room in the building at Spencer Road, where Florence's friend had tried to commit suicide was only a temporary address also, Derek's birth was registered at 37 Selsey Street . This being the address of his maternal Grandmother at the time.

When Derek was two months and five days old he was in the arms of his Aunt Lillian and she was walking with his maternal Grandmother whilst his Mother dealt with her other young son, Arthur.

It was the 7th. of September 1940 and suddenly the air raid warning siren went off, *heralding the first night of the infamous Blitz, on London.* The Grandmother's Sister, Rose had said, in relation to Hitler, "No little jumped up housepainter is going to make me leave my house". So the Grandmother said to her daughter, "You take the baby down to the bomb shelter and I will go and sit with your Aunt Rose."

Aunt Lillian decided to argue saying, "No, I'll bring the baby and we can go and sit with Aunt Rose together." An argument ensued and the Grandmother finally won.

Aunt Lillian consequently took the baby to the bomb shelter and The Grandmother took herself off to her death in her sister's house at number 1 Selsey Street where her, her Sister, Rose Stovell, and rose's Daughter's boyfriend Albert Blake were killed by a direct hit of a bomb. Rose's daughter survived because Albert pushed her under the staircase. *

*Page 89, Wartime Britain- The East End At War; Rosemary Taylor and Christopher Lloyd, Published by Sutton Publishing in association with WH Smith in the year 2000.* Three weeks later aunt Lillian was once again holding Derek in her arms, but this time sitting on the back of a flat back lorry, next to his mother holding his brother, looking for somewhere to sleep for the night. The lorry Driver stopped at a Church and said to the Warden, who was looking after the church, "Have you got room for this lot in your church ".

The Church Warden replied, "No, they are standing up asleep in here, but can you see that school three hundred yards down, well they still had places there a few minutes ago."

The Lorry Driver thanked the Warden and headed for the school. Just before he reached the school there was an almighty explosion as the church received a direct hit and was totally destroyed by German bombs.

# Derek's Tale

During my parents lives their London east end environment was probably one of the worlds most polluted places as well as being a slum.

It was, no doubt, this environment, together with the first World War and along with the very hard life that people had to endure in those days, that contributed to my Mother's personality. She would find many ways, even ironic circumstances, in which she could find an excuse to laugh as though all life was just fun, waiting to be enjoyed. In those war torn days it was often very difficult and, sometimes impossible, to obtain consumable goods, some of which, were considered to be essentials in life. Cigarettes were one item which were often difficult to obtain, some brands more than others.

Living next to the docks had that one bonus, together with the life threatening dangers of course, that some products became easier to lay your hands on, especially cigarettes. I well remember my Mother coming into the home on occasions with American or Arabic cigarettes which had a pungent smell. They were the only alternative available so rather than go without this simple pleasure my Mother would buy them. My Father never woul and when she lit one up my Father would complain and she would laugh and deride him in a gentle and friendly way, even sometimes blowing smoke towards him. If my Father went on a bit too much my Mother would, having been born ten minutes before him, tell him he should respect his elders and stop complaining. This gave her an excuse to laugh once again, though never in a nasty way.

My Mother would use cigarettes to enjoy today because 'you may be dead tomorrow' by courtesy of one of Hitler's bombs we suffered on an almost nightly basis. She got to the state that she was apparently smoking sixty a day when they were available. This, along with the fumes and dust from the destroyed buildings,she breathed in on an almost daily basis (which would have contained massive amounts of Asbestos) caused her to get lung cancer and dying in nineteen fifty six, shortly before my sixteenth birthday. Even if known the dangers from smoking were unavailable to the general populace in those days of minimal communication.

Most communication in those days concerned mainly the war and you were considered lucky if you had only a wireless (Radio), so you had to rely on word of mouth, the newspapers or (especially in London's east end) your own experiences. Very few people, only the very affluent, could afford a rarity like a telephone.

Our family, depleted because my oldest brother had been evacuated to Dorchester in Dorset, spent some time after the destruction of the church mentioned earlier, moving around London and sleeping where we could. My Aunt Lilly told me that it took the authorities, such as they were at that time, virtually two and one half years before they seemed to wake up and decided to send us, as a family, down to Ringwood in Dorset as refugees from the war. My Father doing what was considered an essential occupation as a Fitters Mate in the docks was however kept in London. Also he was used as what was called a fire watcher. This meant that at night during bombing raids he would be stationed on top of a high building with a megaphone. His job was to note where a fire had been started by an incendiary bomb and call down to the firemen to direct them to the fire to ensure it was dealt with at the very earliest moment. Imagine being there and hearing or even maybe sometimes seeing a bomb heading towards you and not being able to even attempt to run away. This must have been as terrifying as being on the front line with the soldiers fighting the enemy.

When we arrived in Ringwood we were sent to a place called Lane End Farm. There were apparently two ladies running the farm as a refugee centre. We heard, though I do not know the truth of it, that the ladies were living with and consequently sheltering two American deserters on the premises. I remember the name of the lady who was apparently the senior person in charge. Indeed I nearly met her many years later when someone asked me if I would like to meet her and her family. I refused point blank and shuddered at the thought. The ladies were living in the farm house and we were billeted in the stables. The bed I remember sleeping in was called a camp bed. It consisted of a metal frame with a canvas sheet spread across the frame and nothing else. I had one blanket and no sheets or pillow and I was expected to wrap myself in the blanket to keep warm.

The entrance to the stables had no door only a large archway and nothing between us and the elements. I was in a stall in an open stable with a piece of sacking hanging across the opening at the front. I well remember looking out directly at the stars in the night sky from where I lay. The water came from a tap against the wall of the farm house and the communal gas cooker was sited on a landing on the stairs. It was in fact an incident at the gas cooker that prompted our early return to London.

The son of this senior person in charge was a nasty piece of work and would take every opportunity to hit me whenever we met. I was just a toddler and he was an older boy. It was not unusual for him to be woken in the night by large numbers of aircraft flying overhead and find his way to the stable and attack me whilst I slept.

Us children would go into the New Forest and play during the day and occasionally would get to ride a forest pony. We would find an apple or something to offer the pony, climb a fence and try to entice the animal to us with whatever titbit we had. If we succeeded we would give it to the animal and attempt to jump on its back. If we succeeded in this we were so light that the pony would sometimes let us remain for a while, if not we came down with a bang. The leaf cover on the ground probably protected us from any real damage.

There was also somewhere close to the farm an ammunition dump. We sometimes went there and climbed through a hole in the wire fence and played inside. One of our companions who played in the ammunition dump had a badly scarred face that looked as if it had been burnt but he had no fear of being there among the ammunition boxes. We moved the ammunition boxes around and made a small enclosure with them. This we referred to as our camp with other boxes we used to sit on.

The problems set up by the son who used to hit me had transferred to our parents. Apparently we were only there for from six weeks to two months. Because of my age my mother was told that she had preference to use the cooking facilities. One day she was making food for me and was using the gas cooker to do it. The senior supervisor came upon her and told her to leave because she said she was going to use the facility. My Mother protested and said, it was her time on the roster and she was making food for me. The woman argued back and pushed my Mother. This resulted in my Mother getting her arm burnt.

When my Father came down on the following weekend he asked my Mother about the bandage on her arm. Knowing the general circumstances, when told what had happened my Father immediately packed us up and took us back to London with him.

Later in the war we managed to find temporary accommodation in Ponders End, Enfield which was north London. The owner of the house, allowing us to take over one of her bedrooms, temporarily, was the owner of a news agents shop. She heard that the owner of a haberdashery shop nearby her shop was looking for a tenant. She informed my Mother and Father of this and arranged for them to meet the owner of the haberdashery shop and we subsequently moved into the flat above the haberdashery. There were at that time still bombs falling and in particular where we were because there was a Gas Production Works opposite and that was a target of German bombers. I well remember the Air Raid Warnings going off and us trooping down the stairs in the middle of the night to sleep in the bomb shelter. The first thing my Father did when we moved in to the property was to get together with some neighbours to erect the bomb shelter as a priority.

One of the first things I remember in a bomb shelter was my second birthday. My family, family friends and people who shared the shelter with us, all decide to give me half pennies for my birthday present. After all, what few shops still existed had very depleted stocks, so there was very little that could be bought with what little money people had. That night, in common with many others, the air raid warning went off and we all trooped down to the shelter to try and get a night's sleep. I however was playing with my half pennies on the floor. Putting them in small piles of varying numbers of coins. Suddenly a bomb dropped very close and the net, very common, occurrence was that many people ended up on the floor with me. Lots of people were in tears from fear and fright caused by the suddenness of it. I also was crying, not from fear or fright, but because my half pennies were all over the floor of the shelter and some had gone under bunks where I could not get to them.

One woman, who was not related to us, we called Auntie Vie, short of course for violet, picked me up and sat me on her knee to cuddle me. When she realised I was crying for my pennies and no other reason, she organised everybody to lift bunks and whatever it needed, to find and retrieve my pennies. When they were all found and given back to me Auntie Vie said, "There you are 'Delboy' your all right now." From then on it seemed my family still called me Derek, Auntie Vie's family all referred to me as 'Delboy' however and others often referred to me in the same way.

Auntie Vie's husband was a very small skinny man under five feet tall. Auntie Vie was not only taller but also somewhat over weight as well. My Father often referred to them affectionately as the long and the short of it, as he did with my Mother's Aunt Bet and her husband Fred.(Great Aunt Bet was a tall matronly woman and Great Uncle Fred was a very short man with a twisted spine.) Auntie Vie's husband was always Uncle George to us children. Unfortunately Uncle George had a problem inherited from the First World War. He had been gassed and was 'Shell Shocked' and consequently had a drink problem and was extremely nervous. I well remember meeting a drunk Uncle George in the street on one occasion after the war, he did not recognise me and the only reason he stayed on his feet was that he was bouncing of the wall as he ambled along.

Uncle George was obviously older than my Mother and Father by at least ten years because he had fought in the first world war which started when my parents were only five years old. His problems manifested themselves greatly when he was in the bomb shelter and bombs were falling nearby. He would shake very noticeably. When Hitler's minions started to send over their Rocket Bombs, things got even worse.

The rocket bomb would begin to impinge itself on your consciousness when you began to hear, very faintly, far off in the distance the sound of the rocket motor. The sound of the motor would get louder as it got closer to you and the tension would build up with it. Sometimes the sound would begin to diminish as the bomb went past you and you would relax. On other occasions you would hear the sound of the motor stop. That was the time when you became desperate to hear the explosion. If you heard the explosion the chances were you were still alive, if you did not hear it you were probably dead.

Poor old Uncle George upon hearing the sound of the motor would start to shake. The shaking would become more and more violent as the sound got louder and if the sound stopped, he would go rigid and not until he heard the bang would he relax. Sometimes it seemed the relaxation that occurred in him was so noticeable it was almost as violent as just before it occurred. On one occasion a bomb had thrown us all out of our bunks and we were all so tired after many bombings that we just crawled into the nearest bunk and tried to get back to sleep regardless.

Me being just a small child and Uncle George being small we ended up in the same bunk. After a short time I became aware of the sound of a rocket motor. Uncle George probably being so tired did not seem to react immediately so may not have heard it straight away. It was not long however before he started to shake. The shaking did not last very long until we heard the motor stop. Uncle George cuddled me to him and said, "Don't worry boy, I'll look after you. "He then went rigid and ended up squeezing me so tight I could not breath. I began to think I was going to die anyway but he finally relaxed and I got out of the bunk and went to my Mother. Years later my Mother was still commenting about the time in the bomb shelter when she could not understand why I did not want a cuddle but would not let her go.

After the war Uncle George was still a part of our lives and used to cut our hair when Dad could afford it. I never told anyone about the 'buzz bomb incident' because I did not want to get poor old Uncle George in trouble.

On another occasion My Uncle Charlie came home, in uniform, on leave (possibly what was called 'Embarkation Leave'). That night he slept in the small bedroom at the front of the flat. The air raid warning sounded in the middle of the night and we all got up and went to the bomb shelter but when we tried to wake Uncle Charlie he, half woke, and said, "Oh leave me alone I'm too tired so I'm staying here." We were not happy but there was no shaking him from his resolve. Directly opposite our flat were two streets of small houses. That night the Germans attacked our Gas Works with their bombs. In so doing they totally destroyed the two rows of small houses. We stayed in the shelter until the all clear sounded the following morning. When we left the shelter we noticed that every ceiling and window in the flat had been destroyed by the bomb blasts and we rushed to see what had happened to Uncle Charlie.

Uncle Charlie was covered in broken glass and dust and dirt from the ceiling, He was completely unharmed and his only complaint was that we had woken him and he had to get out of bed and help to clean up.

When I was three years old my Mother was told, We need you on war work and your son is bright enough that he can go to nursery school. After six months at the nursery school, being younger than most of the other children, I did not fit in, so the decision was made that I should go to an ordinary school because I was creating havoc in all areas. Unfortunately in the ordinary school I was a year younger than the other children in my class so, still not fitting in, I was causing all sorts of problems in the classroom. The Principal said, "He is as capable as all the other children in his class but does not seem to be able to fit in because they are older and bigger than he is."

My experiences at school, amongst a large number of East Enders as well as the locals, and because my name was not a word you would normally associate with the male gender it was easy for my class mates (mates is not really a suitable title for such cruel people as young children can be.) to pick it out and use it as an excuse to bully me.

I began to disassociate with them and the only people I was able to associate with seemed to be the normally social misfits who didn't care anyway. Because of the war there were a large number of inner city children who were from very poor families who had been made homeless by the bombs and who had moved to the comparative safety of the suburbs. They tended towards being misfits because of their family circumstances so there was no shortage of people who might drift into that social category anyway. Some of course settled into the life in the suburbs and had very few problems fitting in.

I remember my first day at school because of a young girl whose name I can still recall but would never divulge. On that day the teacher whose name was something like, although I cannot be certain it was, Miss Farthing, asked us children to do something which was probably designed to make us interact with each other. The net result of this was that most of the children ended up around the teacher's desk but one or two of us stayed at our desks. Myself and the girl next to me stayed. Somehow we became interested in each others bodies. We ended up screwing up small pieces of paper and trying to push them into each others bodies. Naturally I was the most successful and my finger followed the piece of paper it was pushing. I can remember thinking it felt the same as a few days earlier when I, feeling somewhat hungry, had pushed my finger into the nearest foodstuff I could lay my hands on which was a jar of fish paste which had been recently opened. On both occasions I sucked my finger clean to ensure leaving no incriminating evidence on my jumper when drying it off.

This same teacher was our regular 'form teacher' and at a later date in an effort to make us learn to control ourselves, she stated that no one would be allowed to leave the classroom to go to the toilet. A day or two later however I had a minor stomach problem. I put up my hand and requested to be able to go to the toilet. The teacher said emphatically you know the rule so no you cannot, she would not listen further. I repeatedly put up my hand and was duly disregarded so I just let it go into my clothing. A short while later it started to happen again so I started to put up my hand repeatedly again and was ignored. The first time I let it go I had not urinated but this time I let it go again and this time I urinated. The children around me suddenly realised and must have realised also, it was not just me breaking wind which was creating the smell they were aware of.

The Teacher becoming aware also, by way of the behaviour of the children around me, shouted out, "Get this boy's Brother." She then made my brother take me home and that was probably the most uncomfortable journey of my life, especially as my brother made me run the whole distance. The memory of this is just as strong now as it was the next day and this is almost seventy years later as I write it. I might be in what used to be called, 'second childhood' but I am not now restricted by a misguided school teacher so it has not happened again, yet.

In order to get the chronology at least a little correct I must tell here about the day my Sister was born. When I awoke on the morning of 24th January 1944 my Mother, who was already on her feet and mobile because of us young children, told me she had a surprise waiting for me down stairs. I had started school already but I can not remember whether it was a school day or not. My Mother led me down stairs into the Lounge come bedroom of my parents, and there in the corner under the window was a cot and my new born Sister was snuggled up inside. My Mother being clever wanted to make us feel that this was a special day for us all. Of course it was but she wanted to get us very involved in order to prevent any feelings of jealousy later when she had to spend a large amount of time attending to my Sister and seemingly neglecting us.

Me being the youngest was asked the question, "What are we going to call her ? You can name her, so what is it going to be?" She then proceeded to bombard me with suggested names. Each name began with a 'J', Jean, Jane, Jeannette, Joan, Jean, what do you think? I like Jean what do you want, Jean then? Of course she had included Jean more than once and then stated her preference so I said okay Jean. I was congratulated on allowing myself to be coerced without realising and was then lifted up to kiss the baby hello and given a big cuddle. I never ever remember feeling jealous of my Sister so maybe my Mother's ploy had worked and affected me, I shall never know.

I did not enjoy classes where I was with the seemingly 'normal people' and on very few occasions I thought I was doing well but soon found out different. On one occasion feeling good I listened to the teacher at the start of the class and understood what he or she was saying. I consequently did the set work and ended up with other children from the class saying things like, "Del mate how do you do this, what does this mean," etc.. I did my best to explain and during the next break in class they were being just as bad as they normally were.

On another occasion I listened to the teacher because he said something I thought was interesting. It was about quadratic equations and for some reason my understanding allowed me to not only understand the questions given but also when I saw the question the answer just popped into my head. The teacher then set twenty questions for class work and a further twenty questions for home work. He wrote them on the blackboard and strolled across to the window and started to look out.

As he reached the window I said, "I have finished sir." He said, "Do not talk silly boy." I insisted so he said, "Okay boy now do the homework." I said, "But Sir I have done that as well." He then said in an angry way, "Okay boy now bring it out to my desk and we will see the truth of it." I took my workbook to his desk and watched over his shoulder. Every answer was correct but almost without looking at them he crossed out every one and exclaimed loudly at each crossing out (for the benefit of the class no doubt) Wrong, Wrong, Wrong, forty times. I then protested, "But the answers are all correct sir." He then said, "There is no working out."

His job then was to ask how I got the right answers and to follow this up to try to show me what to do. Instead of this he dismissed me and never mentioned it again. I of course dismissed him as well.

This teachers name was Mr. Bancroft, he was a Welsh rugby player and big with it. He had the bad habit of throwing the blackboard eraser full of chalk dust at children in his class. On one occasion even though I was totally innocent he threw the blackboard eraser at me for talking. I had looked at the culprit and as I turned back the eraser hit me squarely in the eyes. Subsequent to this I had to take three weeks off school for treatment to my eyes.

When I returned to school my Mother accompanied me and Mr Bancroft, being our form teacher was holding our first lesson and calling the register. Although he was over six feet tall and my Mother was just five feet tall, she reached up and slapped him on the face very hard. She then threatened him with the hell he deserved if he ever touched me again and he with his very red face could only stand there as she walked out of the classroom to the accompanying laughter of all the other children. One of them even said she hit him so hard you could have got her finger prints off his cheek.

In those days an exam called 'The eleven Plus 'was used to assess eleven year olds. With a view to getting them into what was called a Grammar School. When my turn came round to take this exam my thoughts were, all these people my age are aspiring to go to a Grammar school and I do not wish to be with them. Consequently I did sit the exam because it was statutary but I refused to try and so failed. I thought that had put paid to any chance of my going to University and settled into living with that.

Later I discovered that another exam called the thirteen plus existed. I had missed that because I was in hospital having my Appendix removed. However the school had obtained as pecial dispensation for myself and two others to take the exam late. My Mother was in bed very ill with Cancer at the time and she said to me, "If you pass this exam I will get better and leave my bed to start looking after you properly again." This spurred me on and I tried very hard and was told I achieved some of the highest marks obtained that year.

I lived with the thought that I would know only one or two of the other pupils at the 'Technical School' who were older anyway so maybe I could make a new start and enjoy my schooling from then on. This proved to not be the case and before long, rumours and stories from pupils who knew pupils meant that similar things were happening among the pupils as had happened at the previous school.

I met another pupil who was prone to playing truant and had found a local café where we could spend the day playing pin ball. I joined this boy, Steve, and we often spent our days in the café and eventually found our way to a local Snooker Hall. At the hall we learnt to brush and iron snooker tables and we collected used dishes which got us permission to use the tables and learn the game. We had fulfilled the saying of the day, that a good snooker player was the sign of a misspent youth.

When I was a child I used to suffer quite often with an illness the Doctor called 'Quinses 'which was an inflammation of glands in the neck. When I was nine I had an attack and my Mother took me to the Doctor's Surgery to be examined. The Doctor diagnosed Quinses yet again and while he was examining me my Mother told him she was getting a pain in her left breast. The Doctor started to examine my Mother without dismissing me. He suddenly realised and told me to wait in the waiting room of the surgery. We did not realise at the time but this was to prove to be the start of my Mother's Lung Cancer which would kill her approximately seven years later just before my sixteenth birthday. I had been involved in a few scrapes up to now but I feel this point in time was to polarise in my mind as a time when things began to slowly accelerate in what may be termed my aberrant behaviour. As I said before the children who did not care about my name seemed to be the ones who were somewhat anti - social or not too bright. These were the people who did not look for reasons or question what others did, they just accepted whatever.

Occasionally I had been present when they did unacceptable things but only a fool would question their behaviour so I said nothing and ended up sharing the blame even though I was actually only guilty of watching the act.

As my Mother's illness progressed I found it very hard to be with her and witness her pain and suffering. According to the doctors she could have died at any moment and they even said to my Father, "Whatever she wants, give it to her, she may not get a second chance to get it." This resulted in our getting a television, on rental, to watch the coronation of

Queen Elizabeth the second. My younger sister was deemed too young to see her Mother in such conditions but I was encouraged to go and visit her as often as possible. I took to staying out later and later even staying away sometimes for days or even weeks at a time.

This sort of behaviour upset my family but that did not stop me trying to hide away from the pain. Everybody, even the Doctors seemed to be amazed at my Mother managing to survive for such a long time.

For the last year of my Mother's life the pain was so great that she remained unconscious except for only two occasions. The Nurses told us that on one occasion she became conscious at a meal time so they put food in front of her. She apparently said, "I don't want a wash. Take that away." On another occasion she awoke early in the morning so they put a bowl of water in front of her in preparation for them to wash her and freshen her up. She told them she was not hungry so would they take that away. I was informed by my Father many years later that she became conscious for the last time just before she died. At that moment I was the only member of the close Family who was not there at her bedside. She apparently unwittingly said something which upset the whole Family. My Mother apparently woke and looking around said, "Where's my Derek, he's a little devil but he's the best of the bunch."

My Mother slipped back into unconsciousness almost immediately but my family stayed the normal visiting time before leaving. Sometime after they left, probably in the normal course of their duty, the staff apparently got the impression that my Mother was still feeling the pain of her condition in spite of being unconscious. The Doctor in charge of my Mothers case apparently told my Father that they could do nothing to relieve my Mother so had acted to help her on her way in the interest of kindness to relieve her and us of her pain and suffering. When my Father told us of this he had accepted it and said thank you to the Doctor concerned.

Had I been aware of my Mother's last words at the time, I may have understood what happened a couple of days after her funeral. She was buried on the thirtieth of June and my sixteenth birthday was on the second of July. That was the only second of July in my memory that it actually looked dark and gloomy when I awoke and went down to the kitchen for breakfast. As I entered the kitchen I realised that my feeling that no one would remember my birthday was confirmed, so I decided that I would tell them I understood so that nobody would suddenly realise and feel guilty or upset when they did.

My choice of words was obviously not good. I started by saying, "I suppose nobody has remembered my birthday,". My intention was to say next, "But I understand so don't worry about it, next year will do." Unfortunately, possibly because of my Mother's last words my grieving Father immediately reared up and started to castigate me. He accused me of being the cause of my Mother's death because I had caused her so much worry and stress in her life. My two brother's and my sister stood around nodding and saying yeah, yeah and too readily agreeing with him. I was so hurt and stressed by this I was dumbstruck but in my head I decided that I was leaving home for good after this and would have to make my own way in life without a family. Within days I left home knowing I could always find somewhere to sleep at my best friend's home where his Mother always made me welcome.

My best friend at that time was Leonard Brady and we all, both his family and others, called his Mother Liz, short of course for Elizabeth. When I told her the reason why I had moved out away from my Family she was upset and very surprised by my Father's action's. Being the wonderful person she was, she made me an offer. She said to me, "I could never be such a good person as your Mother was and I could not ever hope to replace her in your life, but if you will let me I will do everything in my power to replace her and I will always be here for you to come to when you feel the need."

Len, my best mate. Circa 1958.

Liz and her family were the archetypal anti- social people who I befriended from school and her husband was in prison at the time and she was finding it hard to cope (partly because she often went to the pub and got drunk). However she was totally sober when she made the offer to me and I shall always love and remember that wonderful lady who in spite of being rough and ready, had a heart of gold. It was to Liz who I turned when I felt I had to get married and needed somewhere to get away from my in laws. Her whole family helped me when I discovered I had been tricked into a bad marriage and needed to remove myself from the situation.

As I said earlier I had watched some activities that were anti - social but only as an onlooker. I admit that on one or two occasions I got involved in some minor mischief but that was all it was because I did not have the stomach for anything worse. I admit that on one occasion I was in a nightclub when I was only sixteen and a group of us decided to go on to a different club. We had travelled to the original club in an old Ford Popular van. About twelve or more of us had crowded into the back of the van and our combined weight meant that the back went down and the front went up in such a way that the driver could not control it properly. The front wheels were hardly touching the road and turning corners was very difficult and fraught with danger. We of course, being young cheered and jeered and egged the driver on to go faster so we could laugh at the antics of the car as it literally weaved it's way along the road. We were so close together in the back of the van that one of the girls claimed she enjoyed being sexually penetrated by one of the male occupants who was bragging about it.

When we decided to go to a different club the driver did not want to carry so many people. One or two had decided to stay and of the rest of us, I ended up getting into a different car, owned by a friend of our driver who had joined us at the club, as the only passenger. The driver of the car I was in went by a different route claiming he wanted to get some more money from his flat on the way. He insisted that he should lock his car and requested that I went into his flat with him. When we got there he made some sexually explicit suggestions to me. I did not know what to say apart from no way but he was big and took up an aggressive stance.

Having been drinking he needed to visit the toilet in his flat so, noticing two or three pounds on a shelf above a fire place I helped myself to one pound for fare as I did not have much money and needed to get to a part of London with which I was familiar. I ran out of the house and down the street as quickly as I could so he could not find me. He however informed the police who traced me through the van driver and when I told my story the police believed me and let me go but still did not prosecute the other man. I never knew why they did not prosecute him.

In my mind I was reminded of this incident some months later when I was accosted by a man who claimed to be a plain clothes policeman. I was leaving a night club and this man approached me and accused me of being a male prostitute plying my trade in the club I had just left. This was absolute nonsense and the girl I was with was in the club waiting for me to return from buying a packet of cigarettes. I told the so called policeman this and invited him to come back to the club where I could prove my case. He refused calling me a liar and said he was going to take me to the police station to charge me.

We were in a dark alley way which led to the club entrance and he had shone a torch in my face so I asked to see his identification. He was not going to show it to me and suggested instead that if I allowed him to have sex with me he would let me go. This convinced me that he was not a policeman so I took my courage in both hands and trying to take advantage of the darkness I pushed him and ran as fast as I could go out of the alley and into a café that we used opposite the club. I was lucky no traffic was on the road, which was quiet at that time of night, because I just ran in as straight a line as I could to the café.

I sat at a table and picked up a menu to hide behind, pretending to read it. I kept looking from behind the menu at the entrance to the alleyway and saw a man leave the alley look around and head for a corner not far from where he stood. I was forced to order a coffee and sat and drank it while I recovered my composure and hoped the man would keep on going away from the area. Eventually When I felt fairly safe I left the café, walked in the opposite direction to the way the man had gone, purchased a packet of cigarettes and took them back to my girlfriend.

Some weeks later I witnessed two uniformed policemen and two plain clothed men attempting to arrest a small fat man on the street and the fat man was proving to be quite a handful for them. I felt certain that one of the plain clothed men was the man who had emerged from the alleyway on that night. In the intervening time many people, both male and female, who were prostituting themselves for money, had told me that they had succumbed to such demands as I was faced with in order to not be arrested for their activities.

Although I had technically left home I kept visiting to see whether the attitude towards me changed at all. Unfortunately I saw nothing of it happening. I did see and get a little involved in my Sister and family being coerced allowing my Sister to be allowed to enter a boarding school which the local council would pay for. The move was coordinated by one of my Sister's teachers who convinced the council that a) My Sister was very intelligent and needed what was considered the extra attention she would get to her education from such a school, and b) it was not good for a twelve year old girl to live in an all male family household at that stage of her young life (approaching puberty no doubt).

On leaving school at fifteen I immediately went to work in a local engineering company that was based in the same building as the Snooker Hall that I had used when playing truant.

That period of my life however was very traumatic, what with my Mother's illness, the way I was made to leave school plus the circumstances that saw me leaving home. I found the Engineering work I was doing was so easy it began to get very boring and I felt restless.

The net result of this is that I left the company and went into the sort of work I felt more interested in. I tried to get work in a Quantity Surveyors office but was informed I needed a number of GCE exam passes that I had not got.

One of the people I questioned about this must have seen something in me and felt sorry for me as well, so he informed me that I could get into a Quantity Surveyors office if I went about it the hard way. When I asked about this he said I had to work on construction sites for six months at a time. I had to work at every trade in construction for six months whilst I took a condensed course on the technical side of the job I was currently doing. He insisted that if I did this and emerged with proof of doing so, no company would refuse me a job. He acknowledged that this would prove to be extremely hard but could be done, but no company would sponsor me to do it so I had to commit myself to the task.

I set out to achieve this and it meant that I mainly only worked in the summer because most construction sites would close in the winter in those days because there were no additives to cement that would allow water based construction to be processed. The problem was that cement, concrete, plastering and related work where water was used would freeze in the initial process and then collapse when it warmed up. The water content on freezing would expand and on defrosting would shrink leaving behind cavities which made the structure weak and it would collapse. So no additives, no cement work.

I managed to get through all the trades but by the time I was at the last stage which was electrical I wanted to get married to my second Wife so I stayed in that discipline to keep a regular income whilst this part of my life went on.

During my learning period I had also studied Bills of Quantities and some of the technicalities that this type of work involved so I found it easy to move into an office where I was involved in estimating and using my technical knowledge. I got myself a job with a cable manufacturing company and spent some years working on Power Station construction. I took classes one day and one evening per week and having got a good qualification which my company had paid for I approached the Director for a concomitant rise in pay and status. I had taken the precaution of finding another employer who was prepared to take me on at a suitable salary but I was very surprised when my company said I was a good and valuable employee but they would not give me any more than I was earning at that time.

I informed the Director of the circumstances (he and I were on first name terms) but he said he did not want me to go but if I insisted then I must choose my own path. The salary the other company was offering was approximately twenty to twenty five per cent higher and I could not refuse it, so I joined their staff.

Having spent a few years with this company, studying technical drawings, learning more about the rules and regulations pertaining to the construction business and gaining experience from all this and site visits, I decided to start working on design and went self employed.

This not only allowed me to earn more but also led to many adventures and experiences, some of which are related here.

# Bob's Woodyard

The flat where we lived in South street, Ponders End, Enfield, North London, as stated before was above a Haberdashers shop. As you looked at the buildings from the road they were in, there were four shops. On the right, on the corner of New Road, was a greengrocers shop, run by the Stanley family who lived above. On this shops left was Bert De Fee's Café, Bert was famous for having been a boxing referee who had met Winston Churchill at a fight Bert was refereeing and had a photo up on the café wall to prove it. Above this shop lived a procession of people, first was the Partridge family, with their daughters Kay and Margaret, who were there during and shortly after the second world war.

When the Partridges moved to Napier, road just round the corner, The Young family moved in. Their children became three, Brian, John and Jimmy in that order although Jimmy was born later after the family moved round the corner to New road where their Grandmother lived. After them another family took over the café and moved in to the flat above I do not remember their name, only that there was the Mother, her son Harry and the 'Uncle?' who ran the Café with the mother. Next to the café was Mrs Williams Haberdashers shop where we lived in the flat above. Next to this was a Co-operative Grocers shop. Above this shop was the Kenny family with two children, Terry the boy and a girl, I think Carrol. Opposite to the four shops, at the back, was the first house in new road, where the Martin family lived.

Next to the Co-op was a corrugated Iron shack behind which was a wood yard. The shack, the yard and two semidetached houses to their left all belonged to Mrs Brown. Mrs Brown sold second hand clothes in the first of the houses, rented the yard to Bob who dealt in timber and eventually turned the shack into a café. When Mrs Brown upset some friends of mine they placed a kipper (A smoked fish) into her tea urn. But it made no difference to her custom and the only fuss that occurred was when Mrs Brown found it and started harranging her customers about it. There were many suggestions as to who the culprits were and among them the right people were named but as no one could be sure the culprits were never apprehended.

On another occasion us children were playing football on the pavement at the side of the café and one of the people who joined in was one of the gangs of children who bullied me when there was a group of them together. He caused some controversy among the players and they gradually drifted away. At the finish he and I were left alone and he was determined to upset me. He deliberately kicked the ball against the side of the corrugated iron café wall and when I told him to stop he threatened me, no doubt thinking I was an easy target. He had disregarded two facts however, a) he was not within the protection of his usual group and b) we were not within the jurisdiction of the school authority who would take note of and punish any wrong behaviour, keeping a record for future reference.

He threw a punch at me which I avoided and I countered with a punch of my own. I hit him two or three times, making his nose bleed and knocking him against the corrugated iron wall. Mrs Brown, having been alerted by the ball hitting the wall and being a little slow moving, now emerged from the café. Seeing my opponent, slumped against the wall, no doubt assumed all the bumping noises were caused by me knocking him against the wall when I hit him. She immediately branded me a vicious thug and told me she was going to report this incident to my mother. No doubt when she did she embellished the story from her imagination and thereby tarnished my reputation even further.

As I said, behind the café, such as it was, there was a wood yard operated by a man called Bob. We Children managed to get Bob to accept us and allow us into his yard. We would help out when and where we could as we watched Bob operating the highly dangerous cutting machinery. When Bob cut the wood into logs we were often given the task of chopping these logs into kindling used to start fires for warmth and cooking in peoples homes. We were shown how much 'firewood' to use and we then bundled the right amount together and tied it with string ready to sell to the customers, sometimes as individual bundles and sometimes by the sackfull of bundles. Logs were also put into sacks to be sold.

Occasionally we also went out with Bob on his rounds to visit his customers and deliver whatever he managed to sell. On one of these trips out, whilst Bob was delivering an order to a regular, he was taking a long time and, getting bored, myself and my companion, John Young, sat behind the steering wheel and pretended to drive. I just played with the wheel but John took it further and played with the gearstick as well. When Bob eventually returned having had a cup of tea, or whatever, he had to restart the engine by cranking the starting handle on the front of the vehicle. Unfortunately, probably due to the worn machinery, John had managed to put the vehicle into gear without operating the clutch.

When Bob turned the starting handle the lorry shot forward and could have knocked him of his feet. Fortunately Bob was a bit nimble on his feet and managed to stay upright but very frightened. He did however get extremely angry and accuse us of playing with the vehicle.

We denied this and accused him of leaving the vehicle in gear. He could not be certain whether he had or not so he just grumbled and started the engine and drove away threatening to never take us out with him again.

On a later occasion, on a Sunday, having once again got ourselves back in to Bob's good books, we were at my home and bored because the weather was bad and we had nothing to do. We decided to let ourselves in to the wood yard where we could be out of the house but in the shelter of the wood shed. This we did by climbing over the gate undetected.

Whilst there we started to feel cold and uncomfortable. One of us, I cannot remember who, decided we could be good Samaritans and warm up the place for Bob for a good start on the following day which was the Monday. So we proceeded to light the fire in the wood burning stove. After all the place was overflowing with wood which had been prepared for this purpose anyway. Unfortunately one of us had been sitting near the fire and could feel a draught coming through the wall near where he sat. This prompted him to cover the offending gap with a piece of sacking. We had built up a very hot fire and, satisfied with that we started playing and ignored the fire for a while. Suddenly there were flames shooting up. We had set the wood yard on fire. We started to try to put out the fire and were very busy when the fire brigade turned up. They sent us out and luckily put out the fire very quickly.

When we were questioned about it we said we were passing and saw the fire so tried to put it out. Our efforts had in fact slowed the fire down somewhat and we were called heroes and praised highly for saving the yard and the surrounding houses. Approximately sixty years later this is probably the first time the truth about the incident has been told. We had not been able to decide between us what to say but although questioned separately we had all said the same thing. There had been four of us, John Young, Buster Clay, Jock ---?--- and myself. As to who put up the sacking which I suspect started the fire I could not tell so we share the blame equally.

John and I went back to the wood yard and started to help Bob again. One day I found a stick which was twice the length of the normal kindling wood so instead of giving it to Bob to cut down to size I decided to cut it down myself using a small axe. This was when I discovered that cutting across the grain was much more difficult than cutting with the grain.

After many attempts I put my finger forward to mark the spot so I got more hits on the same line and, of course, I hit my finger causing me some pain. I still have a slightly misshapen finger nail and a small scar to this day to remind me.

I still have some fond memories of the wood yard and some of the things I learnt about wood and it's peculiarities. Bob was a good man and thankfully we never caused him any other problems but I do remember going to his house one day and whilst sitting on his settee was stroking one of his dogs. I put my face too close to that of the dog and it suddenly seemed to try and bite my face. Luckily I was able to move backwards quickly and I felt it's teeth touch my chin and my forehead at the same moment. There were no marks left on my face but needless to say I never got that close again. I never really understood why the dog reacted that way and can only assume that it was because there was no family member in the room at the time and the dog felt threatened.

# Bread And Spit On It

In September 1939 Great Britain declared war on Hitler and Germany for invading Poland. In London's east end lived a couple, right next to the docks. The man worked in the docks as a Fitters Mate and his Wife spent her time being Mother to their two boys. They both had a great desire to have a daughter.

Having lived through the first world war and, seeing the devastation it had caused within families who lost many male relatives, the pair were very worried that the father would be taken away to war and never seen again. On receipt of the news of the impending war many couples spent every available minute together and in comforting each other created many children. The child this couple produced was not the hoped-for girl, it was a boy who entered the world at the beginning of July 1940 and was given the name of Derek.

When the bombing started the oldest child was sent away as were other children to be refugees and live in the country and small towns that were deemed to be safe as they would not be targets for the enemy's bombs. In this case the oldest child went to a town called Dorchester where he met a girl called Marigold and became smitten with her and spent many years thereafter telling his family and friends about her and how nice she was.

The Father, however, was classified as working on what was called a, 'reserved occupation', in the docks and was not called up to fight like many others. His job was to ensure that boats that became damaged were quickly repaired and sent back to sea to fight for Great Britain in the war effort.

The other two children were allowed to stay with their mother, because they were so young, this meaning that there were three people to house. When Derek was two months and one week old, on the first night of the

24

now famous blitz, the grandmother got killed in a direct hit on the house which was so close to the docks. This left them homeless, and it was made difficult to find accommodation for them so it was going to take a little time.

It seems that the difficulty was such that it made it take so long that they were forgotten somehow, maybe a responsible person got injured or a building housing the paperwork got destroyed.

This meant that the family, apart from the eldest son, spent a large part of the war that ensued living in the East End of London, just a short distance from the city centre and close to the father's place of work.

This put the family right in the target area for the bombs Hitler was aiming at London Docks which was, together with the City and Westminster, a main target for the Germans. This was where the family, living like gypsies and sleeping in a different place each night, began to suffer, like so many others, their bad experiences of the second world war.

The following stories are all true and the one titled, 'The Blitz,' is authenticated in a book, called, 'The East End at War,' by Rosemary Taylor and Christopher Lloyd published and sold by W. H. Smith, bottom of page 89.

Sometime after Derek's third birthday the family were able to move away from the dock area of London and went to live in a London suburb. Unfortunately, the family had been so anxious to move away from the constant danger in the dock area that they moved to an industrial area in a London suburb.

In their new flat they were still being bombarded by Hitler's forces on an almost nightly basis. The father built a bomb shelter in the garden, and they spent virtually every night for the rest of the war, sleeping in there. On one morning they emerged from the shelter when the bombing had been very bad overnight. They had left Uncle Charlie sleeping in the flat, because he was on embarkation leave and claimed to be too tired to bother with going down to the shelter. When they went upstairs to the flat, they found that there were no windows or ceilings left intact, and Uncle Charlie was still in bed and covered in broken glass and dust and dirt from between the ceilings and floors above. When they tried to wake him he complained that he had already told them to let him sleep so they should go away and leave him to it. They forced him to wake however, and he seemed very surprised at the dirt and dust all over him and the bed. He was so used to the noises of war that he did not realise what had happened.

The family was always poor and were used to fighting hunger and cold and the normal degradations of the poor. So much so that the mother's stock saying when asked what they where to eat at the next meal was 'bread and spit on it'. So often was this said that it became engrained into the minds of her children for the rest of their lives. Derek's one and only friend at that time was the son of their family Doctor and at lunch times during the morning break at school, it was not unusual for this friend to give Derek his packed lunch for the day, which was always, Marmite on toast, giving Derek his lifetime love of Marmite.

The combination of the Mother and father, living through two world wars in the east end of London with the dust and dirt, which contained asbestos, from bombs destroying buildings, together with the terrible pollution and the mother smoking many 'easy to obtain' cigarettes, available at the docks, combined to cause the mother to contract lung cancer.

# <u>The Irony of Birth</u>

A few days before the birth of Derek, the family were living in a single room found for them by a close friend of his mother, this friend also lived in the building.

Unfortunately, the Mother's friend was so badly affected by the war that she tried to commit suicide by putting her head into the gas oven. In those days the country was using coal gas and this was fatal if you inhaled enough of it.

Derek's Mother to be obviously upset that her friend was suffering so much she would try to do this. When the friend was taken to the local hospital to be treated the ambulance people and her doctor told Derek's Mother that her friend would be home fairly quickly but may try the same thing again relatively soon.

They apparently said that with the birth of her child being so close she would be better off finding somewhere else to live temporarily until the child was born because this type of stress could be bad for her. The only place available to her was to stay with her Father-in-law in his flat.

Her Father-in-law was the Foreman of a Cartage company who ferried goods all over London. This company used only horses and carts and being

Foreman he was given a flat over the stable where he could keep an eye on the animals out of hours.

This meant that the child, Derek, was born in a stable, which was temporary accommodation for his Parents. There were bright lights in the sky from search lights and other war activities and, believe it or not the Company was owned by three people, the boss, his son and his Brother. This however is where the similarity to another historical character ended.

# The Blitz

Hitler decided to hit London with a massive attack of bombs which would be sustained for as long as possible in order to make the British capitulate. This attack was called, 'The Blitz '.

The first night of the Blitz was on 09-09-1940 when Derek, the family's latest child was exactly two months and one week old.

On the day, Derek's Mother was dealing with his older Brother and so his aunt was looking after him as usual. His Aunt and his grandmother had decided to go for a walk. Whilst they were walking the air raid warning went off, a little earlier than they had expected so they were still out in the open.

Derek's Great Aunt, his grandmother's sister, knowing Adolf Hitler had been a house painter in his younger days, had said, "No jumped-up little housepainter is going to get me out of my house. "So the Grandmother said to the Aunt, "You take the baby down to the bomb shelter and I will go and sit with your Aunt Rose in her house until it's over."

Derek's Aunt argued and said, "No I will go with you and be with Aunt Rose. "The Grandmother argued back and eventually won out over her daughter. The Daughter then went dutifully down to the bomb shelter with Derek and her mother went to stay with her Sister.

That night the great Aunts house suffered a direct hit by a bomb, being so close to the docks, and Derek's Grandmother, Mary Lane, her sister, Rose Stovell and Albert Blake, the Boy- friend of Rose Stovell's Daughter, were killed outright. The Daughter of Rose Stovell survived because her Boy- friend had pushed her under the staircase.

# The Church and the school

In the October, approximately three weeks later, after the death of Derek's Grandmother, the Family were on the back of a flat backed lorry trying to find somewhere to sleep for the night.

As on many other occasions Derek's Aunt was holding him in her arms and his mother was holding the heavier brother.

The lorry stopped at a church and the Driver went in to ask the Warden in charge if he had any room for his passengers to sleep. The Warden had said that he had people so crowded that some were actually asleep, standing up, and supporting each other.

He came out of the church and pointed down the road. He said to the Driver, "Can you see that school three hundred yards down there. "The Driver agreed, and the Warden said, "There was still space in there five minutes ago so you should be lucky there. "The Driver got back in the lorry, started the Engine and set off for the school.

However, before the lorry reached the school a stick of bombs fell and totally, destroyed the church killing most of the occupants.

# Bethnal Green Tube

Derek's Mother and Father were badly affected by this war and spent many nights, first finding and then sleeping in many and varied places. On this day she was close to Bethnal Green Underground station and made note that if anything like an air raid happened, she could seek shelter for her and the children down in the station.

An air raid warning was sounded but she was a little distance from the station at the time and she hesitated because she did not think she could make the distance back quick enough. She was close to a church and made her way there for the duration.

At the station people heard the air raid warning and started to panic. They ran into the station and in their rush to go down the stairs someone lost their footing, tripped and fell and all the other people behind them could not stop in time. Some because they were in blind panic and some because the people behind them in their blind panic were pushing them on.

The result of this was that the first people fell onto the ground and the people behind them fell on top of them and they began to pile up, so they got crushed or suffered other injuries that rendered them helpless with the weight of people falling on to the pile of bodies below.

At the end of this catastrophe seventy people died and many more were injured, either badly or just slightly. Some people were injured, and they considered it only a small injury so, thanking God for their good luck would not have reported it because they understood that priority should be given to the less fortunate others who had suffered much worse than themselves.

Derek's Mother thanked God for her good luck and carried on her life looking after her children and dodging bombs for the rest of the war.

This story could also have been called, 'The Irony of War,' because all those people died without a shot being fired in their direction.

# Bomb Shelter Life

When Derek was born, he was given something and when he considered it later in life, he could not work out whether it was a lucky gift or whether it was a curse. He had a much higher IQ than normal people. His IQ meant that he could, if he wished, join MENSA, the organisation for people with a very high IQ. However, when given the opportunity to do so, he refused for what he considered, were very good reasons, at that time.

What this did for him when he was very young was to notice the behaviour of others and become interested. This interest, because of his experiences in the bomb shelters of the second world war, became a lifetime hobby.

During wartime life tends to be very extreme and consequently people's reactions became very extreme in response.

Poor uncle George, who was no relative but being older was imbued with the title of 'Uncle,' but as it was an honorary title it shall be spelled without a capital letter.

He had been in the first world war and had been gassed and become 'Shell shocked' This meant that his reactions to the bombs and the noise they made was very extreme indeed.

Early in the war his body would jerk with the sound of a bomb and then jerk again, sometimes more than once, seemingly expecting it to be a stick of bombs and he was reacting to each explosion even if it never occurred. His eyes would open so wide that Derek would be ready to pick them up when they fell to the floor. Later in the war when the V bomb, rocket bombs, began to fall his reaction became different. At first the bomb would make itself felt by a very distant and quiet buzzing sound.

As it approached the sound would naturally get louder and louder until it stopped. If you heard it stop you had to hear the bang. If you never heard the bang, after hearing the noise stopped, you were dead. If you heard the bang, you were not dead but may well have been badly hurt.

When this process started Uncle George always reacted the same way. At the onset of the faint buzzing, he would start to shake, and his eyes would begin to bulge. As the sound got louder his shaking and his eyes would become worse and worse. When they heard the sound stop, which happened many times, Uncle George would go rigid and stay like that, with his eyes looking almost inhuman, until they heard the bang when he would relax and start sweating very heavily.

When bombs fell very close to the bomb shelter it was not unusual for some if not all the occupants of the shelter to be thrown out of their sleeping bunks and end up in a big bundle on the floor.

One night this happened and, in the scramble, to get back to sleep, sometimes people would try to get into a bunk that was already occupied by some other person. On this night Derek and Uncle George ended up in the same bunk, but Derek being a child and uncle George being of small stature (less than five feet tall) they just stayed where they were. Unfortunately for Derek the bomb that fell next was a rocket bomb. When the noise of the bomb stopped, Uncle George grabbed Derek and said, "Don't worry boy I'll protect you."

In the short time that the sound of the bomb's engine stopped, and the bang came, uncle George's grip kept tightening and poor Derek, far from being protected, could not breath. Luckily when Uncle George's grip loosened Derek was able to breathe again but he left that bunk very quickly and found his mother.

Uncle George was married to a lovely lady called Violet. auntie Vie, as Derek and his siblings called her, was lovely, gentle and caring.·And incidentally her Husband uncle George used to cut the families hair very cheaply because they, like him, were very poor.

On Derek's second Birthday, in nineteen forty -two, everyone could not give much and, recognising that there was not very much in the shops anyway, each gave him one or two half penny coins as his present.

That night Derek sat on the floor of the bomb shelter playing with his little pile of 'pennies' and making patterns with them on the floor. Suddenly a bomb dropped very close to the shelter and people rained down around Derek.

At the same time his little pile of pennies was scattered around the floor. Auntie Vie had been watching Derek and, being concerned for him, did not cry like so many of the others were doing. She picked him up and cuddling him said, "Don't worry we're alright no one is hurt." Derek was not concerned; he was worried for his 'pennies 'which were scattered and he could not see them all. He said, "Pennies, pennies, "and pointed at the floor. Aunty Vie, realising, stopped everybody in their tracks and almost ordered them to find Derek's pennies.

The hunt stopped them all crying and found Derek's pennies which stopped him crying. Aunty Vie then said to Derek, "there you go Delboy you've got all your pennies back and everybody is happy again." Some years later when Derek mentioned she had used his name to create the name Delboy she said, "No I didn't. I was calling you DELicious BOY.

# Finally, A Refugee

Sometime around his third birthday the authorities finally discovered that Derek and his brother were still in bomb torn London. They got themselves organised and sent Mother and two sons down to Ringwood in Hampshire.

The refugee centre they were sent to was on a farm and run by a woman. She had a friend supposedly helping her. Things started to go wrong from the start. The son of the lady who ran the centre tried to dominate the new children who had arrived because he seemed to think his family, being in charge could say and do as they liked. He would give orders to the other children and expect them to do exactly as he said.

He was four or five years older than Derek and when Derek refused to let him boss him about he got very angry and hit Derek.

Derek still refused to capitulate and from that moment on the son would seek Derek out and hit him whenever he could, even to the extent of coming out of the main farmhouse in the middle of the night.

The lady who ran the centre lived in the main farmhouse along with her friend and it was local common knowledge that they were cohabiting with two American deserters.

The two women lived permanently in the main Farmhouse and the refugees lived in outhouses such as the stable or barns. Derek, his mother and Brother were billeted in the stable.

Barns have doors but the stable had only an arch which was permanently open to the weather. The stalls, where animals were normally situated, had sacking pinned up across the front of each one and Derek could remember looking over the sacking and looking directly at the sky above. Indeed, when they heard planes going over he would look to see if he could spot them. Occasionally he saw the stars being blotted out repeatedly as planes went overhead, but they flew without lights, so he never actually saw a plane, only their shadows, blocking out the stars.

His bed was a single sheet of canvas spread out over a metal frame and he was provided with one blanket which had to go over and under him in order to cover him completely.

One night, having been awakened by the noise of planes going over, and not being able to go back to sleep, he heard the farmhouse door open and shut.

He guessed, correctly, that the boss laddie's son had been awakened also and was on his way to hit him again. He put his feet over the side of his bed and as the sacking was pulled aside he put his arms out at full length in front of his face in a way a sleepwalker had been described to him by someone. He did not know how he should behave and ended up walking around and then, with nowhere else to go, toward the son and expecting to be hit at any moment. The son, fascinated by this spectacle stood aside and pulled the sacking away so Derek could pass through without being awoken.

Derek kept walking and the son followed. What could Derek do now? He could try running but the older boy would catch him easily and probably beat him harder than normal, especially as the son was very familiar with the farmyard and Derek, in the dark, was not. Derek kept walking and went through a gate which led to a slope, and he climbed the slope to a small piece of woodland at the top where the children often played.

Part of the woodland was an almost exact circle of bushes with only grass in the middle and the only way in was open to children to crawl under the bushes but an adult could not.

Derek, not knowing what to do, crawled into the circle and started to walk around it as the son followed him.

Not knowing what to do Derek's mind was racing. Eventually he hit on a plan, he stopped by a gap under the bushes which was easy for him to go through, but he thought the son would have some difficulty. He hoped to be able to get down and get into his mother's bed before getting caught. He turned and pushed the older boy as hard as he could and dived through the gap and ran as hard as he could down the slope.

The next day the family heard that the boss laddie's son had been hospitalised after being found at the bottom of a small quarry that was next to the small circle of trees.

# The Ammunition Dump

Close by to the farm where Derek and his mother and Brother were refugees there was an ammunition dump. The young children would delight in crawling through a broken section of fence and playing inside.

One of the children had bad burn scars all over his face from an incident earlier during the war. This however did not deter him from playing in the ammunition dump one bit.

The children would creep inside because, if they got caught, they would have been thrown out and the fence would have been identified and repaired preventing them from ever entering again.

They would gather as many empty ammunition boxes as possible and build a small square where they could all sit and play at camping. On one occasion they considered they were so far away from any people who were working there that they were able to gather some tree branches that they broke from nearby trees and they even built a roof on the place.

Unfortunately for them, as usual, someone found their camp and when they next returned it had been dismantled.

Curiously enough, although Derek was only there for several weeks, the break in the fence was not repaired in that time.

# Horses for Courses

Once or twice during the time at the farm as refugees the children were able to get as far as the New Forest, which was not too far away.

Some of the local children knew where they could scrump (to help one's self to fruit, mainly apples, that were growing on other people's trees.) apples and on the way to the Forest they would help themselves for two reasons.

One, if they got hungry, they had something to eat, and two they were to be used as bait to entice horses.

Horses did then and still do roam free in the New Forest so were never difficult to find. Once they found the Horses the children would perch themselves on a fence or suitable tree, sometimes in twos, and entice the horses over to them.

They would get the horse into a suitable position and feed the horse and then jump on its back and go for a ride.

There were many spills and falls but being ready for it and it being mostly on thick grass or dead leaves, there were few if any injuries of any note.

# Homeward bound

Shortly after the incident that put the Boss laddie's son in hospital, another incident occurred. It is not known whether the son told his mother of the way he happened to be lying in the quarry with his injuries. It is also not known if the mother decided to keep quiet about it to protect her boyfriend and their relationship.

There was a gas cooker, placed on a landing on the staircase of the farmhouse, for the use of everyone.

A rota had been decided for people to use this facility but Mothers with small children were given preference over others because of the children.

The Boss lady was known for her fractious bad temper and was not very well liked by the refugees in general.

One day Derek's Mother was trying to prepare food for Derek and his brother when the boss lady decided to use the cooker. She walked up to Derek's mother and told her to get out of her way as she wanted to do some cooking. Derek's Mother refused saying she had preference because of the children and it was her time anyway.

The Boss lady got very nasty and started arguing but Derek's Mother stood her ground. At this the Boss lady pushed Derek's Mother and caused her to burn her arm on the gas ring. Despite this she carried on and prepared food for Derek and his brother.

On the following weekend Derek's Father came down to see them. Seeing the bandage on his Wife's arm he asked what had happened. When Derek's Mother told him he wanted to go and strongly remonstrate with the boss lady.

Derek's Mother stopped him saying it would only make things worse. He then said, "That's It, pack your things, we are going back to London where you will be safer. You have come to more harm in this place than all that you have been through in London."

So, the family were no longer refugees but they were back in mortal danger.

# More Bomb Shelter Life

On return to London, in quick order, the family were in the thick of it. One night when they were in a bomb shelter, the bombs were falling thick and fast and very close.

After a night of what some considered absolute terror, the people were totally very grateful that they were still alive.

One man said, "Well let's get out of here and go in and have a nice cup of tea. "He tried to open the shelter door and it stuck after a few inches. He said, "Oh dear, what's this. "He pulled the door back towards him and looked round it and put his hand down through the opening and said, "It's okay it's only a half brick that has fallen. "Having removed it he was able to open the door and walk up the few steps to the surface. When he got there, he looked up and said, "Well, I'm surprised, the house is still there." People started to follow him as he took a few more steps but stopped short and said, "Oh God we are so lucky, I can't believe it."

When they looked, they discovered that the only part of their side of the street that still existed was the end wall of their house and that was not looking too good. Realising that the occupants of all the other houses were buried in the ruins of all their dwellings, which had buried their shelters they all set to work trying to dig them out.

Derek, not really understanding, started to pick up bits that he could carry and put them aside. After a while he found a hand had appeared from under a piece of rubble he had moved.

He shouted to the others as he stood up still holding it and was surprised to find it was only the forearm of someone. People screamed and shouted, "Quick take it off him."

Derek had no real emotion because he still did not understand but he remembered the situation because everyone around him was so emotional, and the woman who picked him up and cuddled him was so upset.

# Uncle Charlie's Close Call

When Derek was about three and a half the family succeeded in moving out of the devastated east end of London and moved to Enfield in north London.

Derek's Uncle Charlie had received a minor injury that was severe enough to have him sent home for treatment. When he was due to go back onto the front line, he spent a couple of days with Derek's family.

Uncle Charlie was allocated to a single bed in the front, and only, bedroom. On the first night there was an air raid. Everyone trooped down to the bomb shelter but when awoken to go with them Uncle Charlie refused saying he was going to enjoy his sleep in a decent bed before going back to hell.

That night the bombing was so bad and so close that the people in the shelter, despite being used to the bombs after such a long time of suffering, thought they would never get out alive. Someone said they would find the building had been destroyed because the shelter had been shaken so many times throughout the raid.

When Derek and his family emerged, they could see no damage because the shop beneath the flat had wooden blackout shutters which were not broken. They went up into the flat and they found that every window was totally destroyed, and every ceiling had completely collapsed. Fearing the worst, they rushed in to see what had happened to Uncle Charlie, who was still lying in the bed totally covered in glass, from the windows and dirty plaster from the ceiling.

They called to him and pulled the bed clothes back a little and Uncle Charlie started to complain that they were not allowing him to get his sleep. At that point some of the dirt and glass fell onto the bed in front of his eyes, and he began to realise what a close escape he had just had. Being cocooned by the bed clothes he had escaped injury.

He then joked in his normal cockney fashion that he would have been safer on the battle field.

On looking out of his bedroom window which was of course bereft of glass they saw that about thirty or forty houses opposite had been, completely destroyed. The fact that there was a small garden in front of the houses and slightly wide pavement walkway, then a two lane road followed by a very wide pavement in front of the shops below the flat, meant that all that destruction of the houses was far enough away to leave the building housing the shops and flats still standing, it had lost all its windows and ceilings but remained intact in all other aspects. The bombing raid had been aimed at the gas production plant next to the destroyed buildings and had the gas tanks been hit the whole area including Derek's families flat would have been just that, flat to the ground.

# War Work and Schooling

When Derek reached the age of three, the authorities told his mother that he was now old enough to go into a nursery and she was wanted to do 'War Work.' A suitable nursery was found and Derek's Mother started work.

Derek however did not fit in well with the nursery. His intellect made him unable to fit in because he had nothing in common with children his own age and was too small for children who were older. He started to cause havoc and upset everyone around him.

The nursery were about to ask his Mother to remove him and this coincided with the family moving up to north London so it became unnecessary.

When the family moved a new nursery was found and Derek started to attend while his older Brother began attending the local school.

Within another six months Derek was back in the same situation he had been in at the previous nursery. A decision was taken. He was just past his third birthday and the schools were about to restart after their summer break. At the beginning of September Derek was to become part of the new intake at the local school. He would be more than a year younger than all the other children but his intellect would carry him through.

Derek's Mother was allowed to take him to school on the first day but on the second day she had to be back at her essential war work.

She told his brother that he had to take him to school and look after him. For a day or two this happened but it was not long before his brother became distracted by something on the way to the school and Derek would often end up arriving on his own.

It was about a mile to walk, but in those days, with most of the men being away at war and there being very little traffic around it was relatively safe for him to do so and he found no difficulty in keeping to the route.

In the modern day in the United Kingdom a person would no doubt be dragged in to court for allowing such behaviour.

On his first day at school Derek sat next to a nice young girl called Mari Peacock who being a year older than him was told to keep an eye on him, he never forgot her as they were together at the school for about eight years and he became friendly with her brother's in later years.

Some weeks later, one of his teachers decided she would teach the children to grow up and be more responsible. She announced in class that too many children were asking to go to the toilet during class so they should stop asking because they should be able by now to hold themselves and go later. She said she would not allow anyone to leave during the lesson regardless.

Needless to say, having eaten a couple of 'scrumped 'apples the day before, it was not long before poor Derek felt the need to go. He knew by his feelings that he would not be able to hold it back so he put his hand up and the teacher remonstrated with him, telling him, he had been told what would happen and she was not changing her decision.

After a few minutes Derek could no longer stop the inevitable happening, so he just sat there and let it happen but did not urinate at the same time. Miracle of miracles, no one seemed to notice, but he knew that he would be in trouble with his short trousers later when he had to stand up to leave the room at the end of the lesson.

However, a short time later he felt it beginning to happen again. He put up his hand again but got a short sharp reply from the teacher. Now he felt doomed so he, knowing it was too late, just let it happen and this time he could not prevent himself urinating as well. It was the urine raining onto the floor that gave him away first and the girls sitting next to him started an outcry which rapidly escalated. This resulted in the teacher shouting at the top of her voice, "Fetch his brother."

When his brother arrived, he was instructed to escort Derek home and return as fast as Possible. His Brother, wanting to get back to a lesson he had been enjoying, ran and made him run to keep up. This, of course, made Derek even more uncomfortable and ensured he would never forget this happening.

This incident became important because it gave the other pupils the excuse to start chiding and teasing Derek and this gave them the further excuse to start questioning his unusual last name. His last name was very feminine and would be difficult for any boy but for an East End boy it was excruciatingly out of place and hard to accept. The teasing rapidly became bullying because Derek would not bow down to the perpetrators, and this was to last for all of his school life.

On occasions his fellow pupils, realising he had understood a particular lesson, would come to him and ask him to help them, but, recognising their shallow dishonesty, he would refuse.

This of course would just increase the bullying when there were more than two of them together, but Derek would still not capitulate. He vowed however that when they all left school he would catch them one at a time and give them a beating for their behaviour.

He achieved this with all bar one who somehow alluded him.

There was an occasion when sitting in a math class something the teacher, Mr. Bancroft Said, alerted Derek's interest. Derek listened and understood the concept at a deep level. So much so that as soon as he saw a problem printed on the chalk board the answer popped into his head without him even having to think. The teacher then set twenty questions for the class to answer during the lesson and on a separate board set another twenty questions for homework. He told the class to start work on the class work and then copy the homework.

Having done this he walked via the window which he idly looked out of back to his chair at the front of the class.

As he sat down Derek said, "I have finished Sir. "The teacher said, "Do not be ridiculous you cannot have. "Derek insisted so the teacher smirked and said, "So now do the homework. "Derek said," I have finished that as well Sir."

The class laughed and the teacher said, "Really, well bring it out to me and I will mark it for you." Derek took his answers to him and the teacher, opening his answer section in his book, began to address each answer. Derek could see the answers over the teachers shoulder and noted that they were all correct. The teacher however took great pleasure in crossing through each answer and loudly said the word 'wrong 'at each one.

When Derek protested the teacher said don't argue with me boy, they are all wrong because you have not shown the working out. There was no attempt to discuss the situation or to give any help the teacher just stopped talking and turned away. Sometime after this in this same teacher's class, a girl pupil, sitting near Derek was talking.

Mr Bancroft a large six-foot three Welsh rugby player, had been wiping the chalk board with a heavy duster.

He turned in time to see the perpetrator was sitting a short distance from Derek but ignored her and, saying Derek's last name, threw the blackboard eraser directly at Derek. As he looked up. the eraser full of loose chalk hit Derek right across his eyes releasing the chalk straight into his eyes. The result of this was that Derek was off school for some time until his eyes healed.

When he was well again Derek's Mother accompanied him back to the school and into Mr Bancroft's (his form teacher) classroom. She, only five feet tall exactly, walked right up to Mr Bancroft looked up at him and raising her arm and jumping hit him so hard in the face that he had a red mark for an hour or two afterwards. She said if you ever hit my son again I will come after you and make you regret it.

Derek Just looked at his shamefaced teacher, kissed his Mum goodbye and took his seat without saying a word.

In those days at the age of eleven pupils took an exam called the eleven plus in the hope of gaining entry to a Grammar school which could lead to a place in a university. It was every bodies aim and desire to get into a Grammar school. Derek however, having suffered so much bullying and getting very little help from his teachers, was not interested in going with a bunch of people who had treated him ill for so long. Consequently, he deliberately failed the exam and, staying where he was, hoped that some of the bullies would leave his life. Later at the age of thirteen another exam came along, the thirteen plus, which could get a pupil into a technical school.

Derek however was in the process of having his appendix removed at this time and his Mother, having seen her brother off to Australia, and maybe (as proved to be the case) never seeing him again in her lifetime, had become more unwell and was bedridden according to her doctors. Derek had missed the chance to take the exam. She somehow communicated with Derek's Headmaster and had secured a promise that Derek could take the thirteen plus alone in his Headmaster's study. She said to Derek please take this exam and if you pass it I will get up out of my bed and walk again.

Derek took the exam, was told that apparently, he got the highest marks of anyone that year and his mother made a superhuman effort and left her bed again for a short time.

# River Adventure One

It was either at the beginning or end of summer. It was definitely not mid -
summer or mid-winter that was for sure. It was one of those days which
was indeterminate, it was hard to tell whether it was going to be hot, warm
or somewhere in between. On reflection I feel it must have been early in
the year, maybe June time.

I had wandered down to the river on my own to try and liven up my
day, after all I was eleven years old or thereabouts and at a loose end as to
what to do. Although I could not swim I had taken my swimming costume
and a towel because I enjoyed playing in the shallows at the side of the
river. This in spite of the occasional lump of human faeces that floated by
near my face. These I would ignore and carry on.

In the event I discovered that a few of my fellows and acquaintances
were at the river swimming. I decided to join them and play in the shallows,
as was my wont. Whilst I played, one of the older boys, Billy Stone, called
over to me and said, "Derek, would you like to play on the other side of
the river?" My immediate thought was, if I was on the other side of the
river I may be able to get to the orchard and scrump (steal) a few apples
for myself. This was something the other boys often did and, if we were
lucky, they would put a few apples inside their costume and give us one
each when they returned, I naturally replied, "Yes, but how do I get there?
" Billy, said, "I will take you over on my back." I readily agreed and we
completed the transfer of myself to the other bank.

I played and explored and discovered that I still could not get to the
orchard because it was on the other bank of a side river that led to the old
water mill. I was thoroughly enjoying myself in my own little world when

I realised it had gone quiet. When I looked up I realised that all the others had left the water and were busy drying and dressing themselves.

I called out to Billy and he called back that he was now almost completely dressed and had no intention of getting wet again because now it was getting cold and the light was fading. No one else was interested and even if they were they probably could not carry me back anyway. I said, "But what can I do, you know I can't swim?" He said, "Well, you'll ave to learn then won't yer." My mental reaction to this was, *O K you flash git, learn is it, well I bloody well will. That will show you.*

Whilst playing in the shallows I had played by standing on one foot, lowering myself so that I was up to my neck in the water, making an arm movement like the breast stroke and, feeling the momentum from this, taking my foot off the bottom and as the momentum stopped, putting my foot back down to the bottom again. This had the effect of moving me a little way through the water.

I practiced this and gradually increased the strength of the arm movement and then slowing the movement a little. This meant that the momentum lasted a little longer. When I gained a little confidence from this I tried making two arm movements. As I gained even more confidence from this I tried increasing the number of strokes. After some long time and when it was dark. I gained enough confidence to attempt to swim all the way across the river. I got so far, panicked, and turned around and swam back. I did this a few times until I suddenly thought, *That last time you actually swam at least half way across, you idiot, and the journey back was the same as swimming all the way across.* My next attempt was a complete crossing and when I made it I was so proud I almost turned round and did it again. But fear of what might have entered the water during the darkness made me get out and search for my Dew drenched clothing, putting it on and hurrying home as fast as I could.

A few months after this a friend and I decided that we would see how far we could swim. Knowing it to be what we considered a quarter of a mile from the nearby lock to the place we called the fifteen arches where we swam regularly, we set off to swim this distance as many times as we could. My friend kept going for at least twelve lengths but a combination of boredom and the fun our other companions seem to be having, caused him to give up and join them. I was determined however and did not stop. I kept on swimming and after the 44th length I decided that it would be more fun to join the others and gave up myself.

I congratulated myself and decided that if I could swim eleven miles at the age of eleven and only then gave up because I was bored, not tired, I must be capable of swimming the English Channel and one day I just might. However I never did try but still feel the confidence to be able to survive in most watery conditions.

Shortly after this, 'long distance swim event,' a new family came to live in the area and within a few months I became friendly with the son who was the same age as myself. I did not know at the time just how interesting this family was, but in the time between this river story and the next I began to find out.

# To Have and Have Not

My other river story came two or three years after I met this family. Like my other friends who were friendly with me because they ignored my unusual family name, these people were somewhat anti-social. I did not know this initially but found it out over time. I met the Father briefly one day when he was bringing in some bags of cement, two at a time from the boot of his car, in order to make a hard standing to become a path down the garden, a base for a shed and a base for a garage. To carry two one hundredweight bags of cement is quite a feat but I watched him do it and was very impressed and admired him for it. I mentioned this to his youngest son, my friend, and he said, "Its in the family." When I asked what he meant, he made a mistake. He told me a story about his Mother's great grandad who had apparently been the World's strongest man who was mightily tough. It seems he came down for breakfast one morning, picked up a teaspoon cracked a boiled egg and died of a heart attack on the spot. To him it was family, it did not matter that the two people were not blood related. The same story was told to me by both his Mother and later by her Father when I met him.

The work my friend's Father was doing was carried out very quick and then for some reason he disappeared from the home. When I asked my friend where his Father was he said, "He is working away." A few days later my friend's older Brother slipped up and asked in my presence what length of sentence his Father had been given. The family treated me like one of their own and I used their house as if it was my own, walking in and out whenever I wanted. I had walked in and they did not know I was about to enter the room where they were talking.

I questioned my friend as to why he had hidden his Fathers whereabouts and he explained that his Father's case had been reported in the local papers. The proceedings were reported correctly, the family address was reported correctly but my friends Father had bribed the police and had his name changed for the prosecution. How he had managed this I did not know but it meant that the family were protected from the resulting publicity as long as nobody realised. My friend was just trying to keep the illusion going for his families sake.

I saw for myself the article in the paper and the Fathers last name was incorrect. The sentence he was given was quite lengthy and unfortunately before the sentence was completed he became ill and died in prison.

The older son was very strong and tough and a good boxer and two years later became a schoolboys boxing champion. He knocked out his semi-final opponent in twenty- six seconds and his opponent in the final in thirty- five seconds.

Approximately three years after learning to swim, on a similar day and in similar conditions I was once again down by the river and the sun had come out and many people I knew were swimming in the river. I did not have a swimming costume with me but decided that I would like a swim. I persuaded a friend of mine to let me borrow his bicycle and set off to my home to get my swimming trunks.

However when I reached a point a hundred yards from the lock I had to stop the bicycle because two young boys were sitting on the towpath and I could not get past them. I said, "Come on lads let me get through." They were half crying and half laughing and in a confused state one of them said, "Save him, save him." and pointed at the river. When I looked I saw a young boy in the centre of the river dressed in what looked like a leather jacket, and trying to grab a log of wood. I found out later that the boy was only six years of age but the log was smaller than his arm and would not support him.

I removed my woollen jumper which my Mother had finished knitting for me a week or two earlier, dropped the bicycle and jumped in the water. I swam directly at the boy, grabbed him by the right shoulder with my left hand, turned and swam one handed to the river bank, holding him out of the water. I tried to put my foot down and lift him out of the water. This was not possible and I started to sink myself so I called to his two friends and asked them to hold on to him until I got out of the water and could get hold of him myself.

Having done this I lifted the boy up and instructed his friends to take the bicycle to the lock house along with my jumper. I carried the boy to the lock house and informed the Lock Keeper and his Wife of what had happened. They furnished the boy with some dry clothing but had no clothing that would fit me. The boys clothing which included the leather jacket which was lumber jack style, tight at the waist, and his boots were put into a bag.

I told the boys friends to make their way home and see the boy later. I thanked the Lock Keeper and his Wife, put the boy on the cross bar of the bike and took him the couple of miles to his home. As I left the lock house I met a friend . I asked him to take my jumper home and explain to my family what had happened.

I later learnt that the reason I could not touch bottom at the point where I tried to lift the boy out of the water was because the river had recently been dredged at that point to a depth of between ten and fifteen feet so that barges waiting to go through the lock could be moored there whilst waiting.

I had forgotten about my pocket watch which was in my pocket but the boys Grand - Father dried it out and repaired it for me. Some time later the Royal Humane Society presented me with a certificate on velum for saving the boy's life.

It turned out that the boy's Grand - Father was a retired policeman. The certificate was presented to me in public by a police Chief Inspector and by pure coincidence it proved to be a police reunion because the Grand - Father and the police Inspector had not seen each other for 27 years when they were cadets together in Hendon Police College.

Between the lifesaving incident and the presentation of the Royal Humane Societies certificate I had changed schools and was now attending the local Technical School. When I attended the School for the first time I had hoped that the problems with my name and the bullying I had received would be left behind but unfortunately not, and similar conditions, although not quite as bad, prevailed.

When The Policeman attended my house to inform us that a certificate was to be presented he gave me an alternative to have the certificate presented in private or in public. I was pretty certain that because the circumstances between myself and the other pupils was virtually the same as before, I did not wish to be part of their establishment. Consequently I had not bothered with doing any homework or even trying very hard at my lessons. This meant that I was probably in trouble with my Head Master.

Not wanting to be expelled publicly from school and making my parents suffer the ignominy of this, (I thought they were probably not aware of my problem at this time) I opted to have the certificate presented in public at school. This was like emotional blackmail making it impossible for the school to sack a star pupil who had given them such good publicity.

However, as things did not change I only lasted one more year at the school. I was then at the age of fifteen and able to start work so I could leave quietly without lots of fuss.

However I made it easy for the Headmaster to make the decision by an unfortunate incident in the school toilets. I had been playing truant with two other boys fairly regularly and managed to remain fairly discreet about it. One of these boys, Steve, who was a little older than myself met me at lunch time one day and said he had some cigarettes and was going to the toilets to have a smoke. I attended in the hope of being given a cigarette for myself. When I arrived I was successful and Steve gave me a cigarette. However Steve had been so excited about having the cigarettes that he had told too many people about them. This meant that there were four or five others there smoking away with abandon.

One of these others was a hanger on with the tough group who thought they were untouchable and were the main school bullies. This boy saw this as an opportunity to prove he was as tough as anybody so he decided to pick on me as his subject. He flicked lighted matches at me and started flicking ash down my coat sleeves. Eventually I reacted and told him I would hit back if he did not stop. He did not stop so I started to fight with him. We were both crouching and trying to hit each other. I threw a punch at his face and my knuckle caught his cheek. I saw his cheek go blue as my hand slid across it, breaking a bone behind my knuckle.

Unfortunately the next thing I saw, mid punch, was the Head Master's stomach as he walked through the door turning towards us. My full weight was behind my fist as I was losing my balance. My fist sank into the Heads stomach and he sank to the floor. With my fist feeling very painful I walked out of the toilet and out of the building. The Headmaster had struggled to his feet and grabbing the other boy by the ear was following me. He followed me along the long drive dragging the other boy by the ear and shouting at me to go back.

I just replied that I had hurt my hand and would need to get it attended to. Unfortunately, it being lunch time and there being a row of factories opposite the school gate, we had an audience of possibly hundreds of factory girls on their lunch break and looking out of the windows at us parading down the school drive. Some of our audience were egging me on and some were egging on the Headmaster. This added to the embarrassment for the Headmaster and fixed the incident even more firmly in his memory. When I returned to school a couple of days later with my hand in plaster because of the broken bone I was summoned to the headmaster's study. After listening to my story that I was defending myself from the other boy's attack on me and in spite of my broken hand, instead of feeling sorry for me the Headmaster told me that if I did not agree to leave at the end of the summer term he would be forced to sack me.

So much for my river adventure saving me, I was now thrown out into the great wide world and had to fend for myself.

# Another River Adventure

As a child from a poor family I only got cheap toys at Christmas and birthdays and my family could certainly not afford to buy things like roller skates or bicycles especially as there were four of us children. My Mother being clever went to jumble sales when she had a couple of pence available. There she would look out for old woollen garments, buy them if she could and take them home to work on. She would add any garment we could no longer use because of Moths or wear and tear, wash them then sit and unravel them and if we were available we got the job of balling up the old wool. This balling up would remove a lot of the kinks in the yarn where it had been knitted up for such a long time. Having gone through this process my Mother was left with the raw material she needed to start knitting various items of clothing for the family. Some of these items, having been washed yet again, appeared at Christmas as presents and if one of us had a pressing need for some item we were given it as she manufactured it. As a consequence of our poor status, if we wanted to have things such as roller skates, bows and arrows, fishing rods or bicycles we would have to make our own out of second hand materials if we could locate them.

We could locate such things if we were prepared to scrabble about in the local council dump until we found what we required. We then cleaned, repaired and assembled the parts to produce the item desired. Often we had to make do with items that we could not repair. This meant that things like bearings used to make a crackling sound as we used the item. Sometimes when we were lucky enough we found two of the required item and then we would open them up and cobble together from the parts a usable object that made less or even no noise as we used them.

When I was eleven, shortly after I learnt to swim, I had been to the council dump on yet another foray and finally found enough bike parts to put together my own bike. I assembled the machine and after testing it I started to use it to get further afield to broaden my adventures. One day I rode my bicycle down to the local lock on the river Lea to watch the boats that used the lock to raise or lower themselves in order to continue their journey along the river to their destination. The destinations mostly being either somewhere on the river Thames where the river lea ended or at Brimsdown or Enfield lock where the industrial areas were. On this particular day I noticed a lady I had seen before and being a little familiar with her face and presence I easily responded when she spoke to me. She started with something like a passing remark about the weather or some other innocuous comment. She then continued until she mentioned the fact that my bike was a girls frame and, did it belong to my sister or a girl friend. I explained that it was the only frame that became available at the council dump.

This gave her an excuse to ask, in a nice way, about the circumstances and then to praise me at my cleverness. The flattery obviously kept me interested and then she mentioned the heat of the day and suggested that we find some shade to continue our conversation in a more pleasant circumstance. I of course agreed and she led me away to sit behind some large bushes at the other side of the field well away from the lock. We laid down our bikes and sat talking until she shifted her position and ended up with her head on my lap. She made the excuse that the sun was hot where she had laid at first and I never checked or even thought about it. Thinking about it later I realised her head suddenly became animated in a way it had not been before.

Her head movements had an effect upon my body and she then said, "What is that lump ?" and put her hand on my penis. At this she expressed surprise that I was such a big boy for my age and that she had not seen something so big on a boy before. I being surprised and delighted at the turn of events just carried on and started to enjoy our encounter even more than I had been. This obviously led to us carrying out some sexual acts, which we both seemed to enjoy to the maximum, and at the end of the day she surprised me even more by insisting we arrange to meet again very soon. This led to an affair between the two of us that lasted from me being eleven until I became thirteen. At some point during our affair I discovered that she was twenty six years old and that she had been raped when she was younger by an Italian prisoner of war that she had come into contact with by some means.

When I was about five or six and out buying cigarettes for my Father and Mother one day I had come across some of these prisoners who I assume had been allowed to roam the streets because the war had ended and they were waiting to be repatriated back to Italy.

They had been very happy and nice to me whilst they and myself purchased cigarettes. I frustratingly forget the ladies name but during our affair she, having studied a lot, taught me probably a lot more about sexual activity than many adults knew in those days.

She told me that she hated the rapist and the circumstances (maybe partly because he was at that time an enemy of our country) but she could not forget some of the feelings she had gone through and had felt compelled to find out more. The fuss and emotion that she had experienced and the haunting possibility of being pregnant because of the rape led her to try gaining her experience from people who she thought were too young to get her pregnant. She actually said to me one day, "You can't get me pregnant yet." We did not have full sex every time we met, it was often oral or by hand, but we never used condoms or even bothered to take precautions.

We used to go for rides to many places and shortly after my thirteenth birthday we had been out for a ride and on the way back we were to go down a hill known as Friday Hill in Chingford. The hill is very steep and we were just freewheeling down the hill when my cheap (One Shilling and six pence in the money of the day, seven and one half pence today) mudguards on my bike decided to fold up because of the vibration and wound themselves into my wheels. I managed to stay upright and stop the bike but my companion stated that she could not stand it any more because I took too many chances on danger, she mentioned my pulling a young boy from the river Lea as one case in point. She said we had to end our relationship and would not see me again. I never did see her even down by the river where she said she loved to go. But I realised later that this was only an excuse to end our relationship because I had reached that dangerous age and she was already taking chances on getting pregnant before we stopped seeing each other.

I will however be eternally grateful to a beautiful and physically lovely lady who looked for a solution to her personal problem in such a way as to do no harm to me personally but taught me more than any academic programme was going to do. This included life skills as well as anything else. I desperately hope she found happiness and if she ever reads this; Please feel no guilt or worry about me or any other companion you may have found because I am sure your attitude and behaviour made your relationships good and harmless. Thank you from the bottom of my heart.

# Spitter Brown's Mate

In the modern world of 2013 young children entering school know more than their parents did when they entered school for the first time. Reasons for this are things like the parents passing on to them, from day one of their lives, the greater knowledge that their parents have gained from the Media (which is rapidly shrinking our world into something like a small village was one hundred years ago). The media continuing this barrage of information on a daily basis and the greater ability that everyone seems to have gained to communicate information that the child may have otherwise missed because they were not interacting with the media at the time it was broadcast.

When I was a child in the late 1940's and early 1950's that gap in knowledge was probably smaller but nevertheless still existed to some extent. In those days technology as we know it today was almost non - existent and was definitely not available to the public like it is today.

Because of the Second World war which ended in the mid - forties there were many poor people trying to get along and many rebuilding schemes and updating schemes which created building/demolition/repair sites throughout the country. Hence it was not unusual to see various sites with a small hut or tent on them where a night watchman sat guarding tools, materials and constructions or excavations.

On one such site my friends and I became friendly with the night watchman so that we could stand round his hot coke brazier during the early evening and keep warm when it was too cold to play the games such as 'Hide and seek' that we amused ourselves with before our parents called us in to go to bed. Sometimes the Watchman would join in a street football game we organised between ourselves close to his site.

We considered people who could afford radios (We called them wirelesses) to be well off which we were not, and televisions were almost completely unknown items even for some rich people at that time. In fact I believe that television was only reintroduced in 1947, having been a failure in 1936 when they first tried it out. This meant that indoor games such as quizzes or drawing or 'I spy' were the only recourse we had to any entertainment in the warm. The noise we made would disturb the very young who were trying to sleep in whatever small dwelling we shared, indoor telephones were also a rarity at the time, so we ended up playing in the street until our bedtime came along.

Our watchman's last name was Brown, I cannot remember his first name because we called him 'Spitter'. This nickname came about because he feigned a nervous habit which he claimed was caused by his war experiences. This meant that he was able to claim some sort of 'War Pension'. His 'Nervous twitch' had him suddenly turning his head to the side very quickly two or three times and on the last turn he would spit to the side.

We were convinced it was put on because a) he never spat on anyone except once or twice on the person who was sent to investigate that the twitch still existed, and b) when he was very involved in some activity that interested him he seemed to totally forget the twitch was meant to be there. There seemed to be no consistency, but it was enough to supplement his very poor earnings from being a Night Watchman. In later life I felt that spitter confirmed he did not really have an honest twitch because I realised something quite significant. At that time I used to meet him occasionally in the local snooker hall. One day when a person, whom he told me he could not stand, was persistently in his company he had a sudden twitch and spat on the persons foot. When he did this I realised that although he twitched in the Snooker hall, he never did whilst playing snooker, and when he had done this in his night watchman's tent or hut he never produced any spittle unless the fire was there to produce a dramatic sizzling affect. However when he was outside the evidence was left on the ground where he had stood.

On nights when people who lived nearby complained about the noise we made chasing a ball about he would regale us with his war experiences. More so when he realised our bed time was imminent and he wanted to keep our company before the long night claimed him for his work. Sometimes he would talk about other things he thought were interesting and on one occasion, when one of our number had been badly treated by a so called friend, Spitter recalled an incident he claimed occurred in his own life.

When he left school, in common with most poor people of his day, he had no qualification to do anything other than labouring. He was lucky enough however to get himself a job and set off on his new life. When he received his first pay packet, just like his friends and colleagues of his age he went straight to the public house to celebrate. At the end of the following week he found he was struggling to buy enough cigarettes and his lunch. The second week was just the same. After two or three more weeks he started to question his actions. After his deliberations he decided to spend less in the public house each week in the hopes of making the end of the week easier.

This he found not too difficult to achieve and after two weeks of his efforts he found he had a little spare cash in his pocket when he received his pay packet. He decided not to spend this cash but save it in his bedside drawer. He kept this habit up and one day he checked the total and found he had saved ten shillings. (50 pence in todays money)

In those days, that was quite a lot of money, almost one weeks wages, to have doing nothing in a drawer. It gave him impetus to keep doing what he had been doing and made him feel proud. He was somewhat street wise and only told his Mother and his best friend. He kept trying and occasionally purchased an item like a new shirt for the weekend. He boasted to his friend that he could always lay his hand on a pound when he needed it.

One day his friend was noticeable by his absence in the public house on the Friday night. Thinking his friend may be ill or otherwise indisposed, Spitter went to his friend's house on the Sunday and his friend's family told him his friend was out with his 'young lady,' as they put it.

Spitter did occasionally see his friend mid- week and they enjoyed each other's company even though the main conversation seemed to revolve around his mate's girlfriend. Then one Friday evening his friend came to the public house. He seemed somewhat distracted but stayed all evening and got quite drunk. He seemed so incapable that Spitter decided to accompany him home to ensure he arrived safely.

Having arrived at the house his friend did not want to go in, so Spitter stayed with him and his friend eventually summoned up the courage to inform Spitter that he had made his girlfriend pregnant. In that day and age it was not too uncommon but it was very frowned upon and the people involved were often castigated by all and sundry.

Eventually his friend did go into the house and Spitter was left to wander home thinking about his friends plight. A week or so later Spitter's friend told him that a relative of his girlfriend had offered him a job some distance away. The idea was they would get married and present themselves as a married couple to people who knew nothing of their past history. They could initially stay at the relative's house until they could find their own place and settle down.

The problem now was that they needed money to achieve this and Spitter was the only person they knew who had any available cash. At that time Spitter had just over five pounds in his bedside drawer. Up until this point Spitter had not even met the girl so his friend arranged that they could meet together. The girl was on her best behaviour and presented herself so well that Spitter found her very charming and easy to like. Spitter was so taken with her that after a few drinks he told them how much money he had. When he mentioned this they said they may manage it with that amount although they really needed more. The couple made a very good job of convincing him that his money was very little in comparison with what they needed. So, in his cups, he promised to lend them the five pounds even though his better judgement and feelings made him feel uncomfortable about the whole business.

In the event Spitter not only lent them the five pounds but he also added some money to what was left in his drawer and gave them a wedding present. With regard to the wedding they said, because the money was so little they were forced to get married in the country place they were going to, which was cheaper, and they had to keep the guests down to parents and the relative who was helping them.

It was a working day when they travelled and Spitter never saw the going of them.

Whenever Spitter went to see his friend's family there was always some reason why they could not tell him where the couple were, bad feeling with the relative, so they were about to move, they were having trouble with their rent so would probably have to move again etc. etc..

Spitter never saw his so called friend or his five pounds ever again. The bitter lesson that Spitter said he learnt was that you should respect other people but never trust anyone enough to lend them money.

# Mott Kettle's Luck

In my attending at Snooker Halls as they were called in my young days I met many interesting people. One person I met from my childhood had been the man we called Spitter Brown who I have written about in a different section of the book.

I also met a gentleman we called Mott Kettle. What his true name was I could not tell you but this is an interesting story I know is true of this man. One day, as was his wont, Mott came round the hall asking people to lend him some cash to go to Walthamstow Greyhound Racing Track . He had already been offered a lift to the track by an associate of his but had no money at all to bet on the races with, which he considered an essential.

Most of us he asked had no money to lend, others did not trust him to give it back whether he won or lost. However he managed to get someone to lend him Half a Crown, That was two shillings and six pence in the money of the day and is equal to twelve and one half pence in todays money. Little as we now think it is, that was a reasonable amount in those days and being a Wednesday Mott was determined to liven up his midweek.

Mott had a plan. On arrival at the track in time for the first race, Mott placed a bet of the full Half a crown on his favoured Greyhound. The dog won and Mott proceeded to put all his subsequent money on every race of the night. So after each race he placed every penny in his pocket on a dog in the next race.

Every dog he picked throughout the evening won its race and after eight or ten races Mott had a large wad of notes in his hand. (Some said as much as three thousand pounds, which given the odds on each animal it could have been) He returned to the Snooker Hall triumphant and even paid back the money he had borrowed. He proceeded to play Snooker and then cards and bet on the horses the next day. On the Saturday he came into the hall without a penny to his name and went round trying to borrow another half a crown because Walthamstow dogs were open again.

Mott had the type of personality it was hard not to like. His thought processes were simple and direct and he could smile through his problems whatever they were. In spite of this people thought him not worthy of their trust. They seemed to view him as a likable, ne'er do well. Later in life I questioned a friend who confessed he had lost every penny at the 'dog track'. My question was how did you get back home with no money, did you walk ?

The answer came back as a derogatory "No, I just jumped over the back fence of an 'Off Licence', nicked a crate of empties and took them in the front door and got the money back on the bottles". In those days drinks were sold in glass bottles and the companies gave money back on the empty bottles to save buying expensive new ones. The fact that the shop (Off Licence) who sold the drinks in the first place had already given someone the money back on the bottles seemed to amount to nothing in the consideration of these people. When I asked my friend where he had learned this trick he just said, "Mott Kettle".

Some few months after Mott's winning and losing so much money between Wednesday night and Friday night of the same week I heard that he had been apprehended stealing copper from outside a factory in the vicinity. Apparently Mott and an accomplice had swum across a river, released one end of a barge full of copper and pushed it across to the other side, tied it to a tree to hold it stable and started to unload it into a van. The factory night watchman had heard them however and had called the police who caught them red handed.

# My First Marriage

I was out with Friends having a drink and trying to have the best fun time I could. I met this woman who did not seem to notice me at first but her female companion spoke to me whilst I was at the bar of the establishment we were in, buying drinks for my companions.

The friend asked me if I needed help to carry the drinks I was getting. I refused what seemed to be a genuine offer but, having noticed her companion earlier I invited them to join us, hoping my companions would like the idea.

My companions did like the idea and the three of them started to vie for attention from the ladies. I was busy clearing glasses to make room on the table we were at and one of the others went to the bar to buy drinks for the ladies in spite of the fact that they had full glasses having just purchased their drinks from the bar. When I finished what I was doing this woman I had noticed earlier was looking at me and started to talk to me. She made a point of sitting next to me and we started to get on famously.

The chap who had brought the ladies unnecessary drinks at the start complained at one point that myself and this lady were acting as if we were alone together. We apologised and started to include ourselves in the general chat. Having found out the ladies name immediately and liking her so much I was totally pleased when at the end of the night she asked me to walk her home because, 'the street lights down her street were not very bright'.

Her name was Valerie. I decided she was not quite as bright as the lights in the street where she lived but she had a good personality and was very nice to me. She insisted on a second date which we arranged that night. On our second date we were alone had a marvellous time and at the end of the night she was very accommodating. I decided that we would keep our relationship going in the hopes that it would last a while before something happened that would cast a shadow on it and maybe end it. The reason for my thoughts were that I seemed to be a nearly man and came second too many times in anything I did.

We ended up seeing each other every day for every hour we could and I was being very careful that I did not slip up in our intimate moments which were many. Then one day came the bombshell, she was pregnant, I was astonished and disbelieving.

I was so disbelieving I went round asking questions of everybody I could think of. Every answer came back pointing at me being the Father. Even though I was sceptical I could not prove otherwise so I decided to be a gentleman and marry Valerie hoping she would be mouldable into a good wife. We lived with her family for a short while but things happened, which I will relate later, that made me uncomfortable and so I decided to move us out with the excuse that we would need more space when the baby arrived.

I rented a room in my best friend's mother's home which was a bungalow. Valerie carried on working for a short while and I worked hard to ensure we had sufficient money coming in. I managed to get a job in a precious metals refining company. It was shift work, three shifts spanning twenty four hours in the day, and it was extremely tough. Employees were graded to reflect their importance to the company and the hourly rate they were paid. I managed to get myself graded high very quickly and received a good wage each week. The company ran seven days per week and because of the way the shifts were changed at the end of the week and because the work was so tough it was not unusual for operatives to ring in sick and not start their first shift of the week.

This meant that at the end of the week when your shift ended it was not uncommon for the foreman to ask you to stay on and do a second shift with a short break in between. If you were graded higher than your comrades you would be more likely to be asked than anyone else. This meant you worked sixteen hours if they could not contact the operative on the next shift and ask him to come in four hours early. On at least two occasions I even worked twenty four hours and ended up changing shifts for a week in order to get eight hours of rest in between. It was also not unusual to be contacted and asked to go in four hours before your own shift to make up for the man who had not turned up for his first shift.

I was earning very good money at this job and tried giving my wife enough money to last the full week. Unfortunately this did not work and she would be asking for more money on the Monday, so I resorted to giving her a daily amount with the amount being a little higher to allow for Saturdays weekend shop. There were, unfortunately still problems and my wife claimed she was buying tobacco for her Grandmother who preferred to make her own cigarettes. I therefor increased the amount I gave her and later discovered that whenever possible she was buying shopping for her Mother, Sister and Grandmother and I was virtually keeping the whole family. This of course created some problems and friction between us.

When the baby arrived I of course gave it high priority and did my best to ensure it was treated and fed in the proper manner. My Landlady was a wonderful person and did her best to help out but she could not always be there. One day when the child was a few months old my wife tried to feed it cold milk and was unhappy because the baby would not drink it. I told her she should have warmed the drink up and her reply was to throw the bottle at me and say, "Shut up, it's not your fucking baby anyway." I was very unhappy at that but not too surprised. I asked what she meant but she was not forthcoming. Eventually she mentioned the foreman where she had been working. I told her she had better go back to living with her Mother Until I found out the truth of the situation.

Within less than a week she was back and not wanting to leave again. I was unhappy at this and tried to think what I could do about it. I realised that my Brother's upcoming wedding might be an ideal situation. An idea came to mind but would need some excellent stage managing in order to pull it off. The type of 'Rock and Roll' Jive dancing that I did was very taxing, especially on the feet of the woman with many fast twists and turns. I bought my Wife a pair of very fashionable, very high heeled shoes knowing she could not resist wearing them to the wedding.

I acted very moody and bad tempered when I did this, saying to her, "No wife of mine is going to turn up at my Brother's wedding looking frumpy and down at heel.

The night before the wedding I hid my Wife's low heeled shoes and left the new shoes by the side of the bed so she could not miss them. When we got out of bed the next morning she started to get ready but realised she would need her low heeled shoes if she wanted to dance. She started looking for them and this gave me the chance to start winding her up.

Unfortunately she eventually found her shoes so I told her to put them in her bag to ensure she did not lose them again. When she did this I took my opportunity when she was not looking to remove the shoe and hide them once again.

At the wedding festivities there were two of my Sister's friends who were unattached and attractive so I made sure to dance with them all the time. One was slim and the other slightly plump and infinitely, in my opinion, more attractive. She was the one who got the most dances. My dancing so many times with them made my Wife upset so she insisted on dancing with me, in her high heeled shoes, and made her feet sore very quickly. She tried dancing without shoes but the floor made this very uncomfortable. On one occasion when one of my Wife's favourite songs came on she asked me to dance and I said, "Sorry but I have already booked this one with Pat," the plump one of my sister's friends.

At the end of the night my Wife was very upset and tried to argue when we arrived at our room. I refused to talk about it at two in the morning because I did not want to upset our Landlady or her family by having a shouting match. In the morning, when we got out of bed my Wife started to get angry all over again and I did not help, my responses were meant to make things worse and they succeeded. She eventually took up the baby and left saying she was going back to her Mother.

I packed all the belongings of her and the baby in a large suitcase. I said to the landladies oldest son, "If she tries to come back while I am out, do not let her in and hand her the suitcase and tell anyone who asks that she only came back to collect her belongings." She came back with her brother and my instructions were carried out to the letter. I had given the land lady three weeks rent and gone back to live with my Father.

A few days later I went to the place where she had been working and pretended I had just met her and was interested in starting up a relationship with her and asked if they knew where she lived. When one of the other women working there realised who I was referring to, these were her words to me, almost verbatim. "The only reason why the dopey cow kept her job here was because she was having sex with the Foreman during our dinner break. What's her baby like have you seen it ? He pretended he did her a favour by letting her stay full term until the Doctors told her to leave. But me and a few others are sure he only let her stay to keep getting his leg over and prevent her telling the Manager what had been going on."

I had not ever contemplated divorce previously and did not know what was involved in marriage breakups. I was advised to go to the 'Citizens Advice Bureau (CAB)' which I did immediately. When I got there I encountered a note on the front door saying closed for annual holiday back in three weeks and dated the day before. Two weeks later, 8th August 1960, was the first anniversary of our marriage.

The law at that time said, If a marriage broke down irretrievably within the first year it could be annulled immediately without ceremony. Not knowing this I waited until the three weeks were up and approached the CAB again and was advised to apply for 'Legal Aid' and see a solicitor. Nobody advised me any different and with divorce being difficult to obtain at that time, it seemed Solicitors saw this as a money spinner and it took me five more years to obtain. What I was not advised at that time was that even though I received 'Legal aid' I was obliged to pay back any costs involved, after the event.

The Solicitor insisted that I needed irrefutable evidence even to apply to the court in the first instance. He did not try to help me obtain that evidence but left me to obtain it any way I could. It was not long before my wife applied for maintenance for herself and the baby. When the court hearing for that was set I refused to let the Solicitor near it and insisted on talking for myself. By now I was beginning to suspect the Solicitor was only interested in making money and I was only tolerating him because the law insisted I have him on board.

On the day of the hearing I managed to get my wife confused and talked her into admitting, first that she was working and her Mother was her unpaid baby minder because she was idle during the day anyway and second that I was not the Father of the baby and had been tricked into the marriage . The Ruling Magistrate threw the case out of court saying I had no responsibility to either the mother or the child. I must admit to feeling guilty at leaving the child in the hands of this woman and her family but had to steel myself into not becoming a dupe for them.

In the next five years I went through some risky adventures as an untrained detective trying to obtain the necessary evidence to get the solicitor off his backside and into the court on my behalf. One must remember I was only just nineteen when I married and only twenty five when I finally obtained the divorce.

During the marriage I had been put into some very difficult circumstances by my in laws. On one occasion one of my Brothers-in-law who was married came to me with his very attractive and sexy wife and requested that I make love to her in front of him and show him how it was done because my wife was already pregnant so I must know what to do and when he knew, he could get his wife pregnant. What I actually did was to explain exactly how he should go about things and he said he did not penetrate fully because he was afraid of hurting his wife. I said that full penetration was an absolute necessity and it is a little sore at first but then his wife would absolutely love it and even demand more. I also explained that if he saw me do that he might have hit me thinking I was hurting his wife badly and sometimes women fall for the man who deflowers them and turn away from other men completely. Consequently they had a beautiful baby and named it after me.

On another occasion my wife and I were thinking we were alone in the house and were having sex in the bedroom when her, slightly older, sister just entered the room settled on the bed next to us and seemed to ignore us and go to sleep. Somewhat taken aback I said to my wife, "What a cheek, I have a good mind to put my hand up her skirt and give her a good seeing to." My wife replied, "Go on then I dare you." I of course did nothing of the kind but feeling a bit put out to say the least we carried on to a finish. She did not stir and we dressed and left the room.

On another occasion My Mother-in-law sat on the sofa in front of the television and it was an extremely hot day so she said she felt like taking her top off. My wife said, "Well, go on then Del won't mind." She did so and her left breast had fallen out of her bra. Everybody laughed and she unabashed took her time replacing it and said, "There you are Del that's a little treat for you."

On another hot day shortly after this incident all the family were in the garden enjoying the sun and there was a programme on the television I wanted to watch. I went in and turned on the television and settled down to watch. Within a short matter of time my wife's very sexy fifteen year old sister entered the room and sat opposite me. I looked up to say something and she was sitting with her knees in the air, facing me and wearing very loose knickers exposing everything. At that time the age of consent was something like eighteen so again I managed to do nothing and when I did not respond she left the room and went up to her bedroom.

On yet another occasion the slightly older sister was making fun of me and making jokes on my behalf. This was something that was just harmless fun and I joined in making fun of her.

After a while she said she was going to take a bath and warned me not to go in there as she would probably break my back. The family bathroom opened off the kitchen downstairs and we could hear her from the lounge because she had not closed the door. She eventually said she had finished and anyone could now use the bathroom. I had wanted to urinate so when she did not emerge, thinking she must be standing in the kitchen, I went to the bathroom. When I entered the bathroom she was standing in the bath with a towel held in front of her. She had complained two nights before about this towel having a large hole in it and now she was holding it as if to shield herself but, giggling, she had the large hole strategically placed so that her entire pubic area was in plain sight for me to see. I apologised and left the bathroom immediately.

It seemed the family had a very carefree and almost innocent attitude to this sort of thing. Indeed, the oldest brother and the fifteen year old used to go upstairs every Saturday and change half the bed sheets every week. The family used to make comments about this because of the length of time they took, but initially I used to ignore what they said. Now I became more aware and started to take the comments to heart and decided we had to move out. Later I felt that this attitude they had might be their undoing so decided it could be useful in getting my divorce.

On one occasion after I started searching for evidence for the divorce, I was informed by a friend that an acquaintance of his had been bragging in the public house of finding a woman, who he had met in the pub, who was very accommodating in the bedroom department. My friend felt that it may be my Wife because the Pub they used was the one my wife and her family frequented so I asked my friend to introduce me anonymously to this person. When we were introduced I encouraged him to tell me about this woman on the pretext that she may have a friend I could meet.

He named and described my wife very accurately then compounded this by naming the road she lived in. I knew of no other person with this name, or of this type in this rather short road so I pushed for more information. My Mother-in-law was nothing to write home about, she had something like about eleven children and the three oldest at least were older than my current companion. Her body had migrated somewhat south and she had a mouthful of Black stumps for teeth. My companion boasted that he had, on more than one occasion, spent the night lying between my wife and her mother and boasted that he moved from one to the other throughout the night having sex many times with both of them.

Being somewhat naive I then informed him who I was and that I needed the information he had just given me to get divorced from this woman. Needless to say I never saw him ever again. After this disaster I went to the same public house again one day. On this occasion I stood in a shop doorway to await her arrival, after she arrived I waited to give her time to settle and then entered the bar where she was most likely to be.

Sure enough there she was sitting in a seat next to two men and they were chatting animatedly together. I went straight over and faced them when I accosted the two men they seemed embarrassed and tried to leave. The first one to attempt to stand was a huge man at least six inches taller than me and bald. I could not afford to let him reach his full height because he would have just brushed me aside and maybe have injured me and or started more aggression from the drinkers around us, so I pushed him back down very quickly. He appeared to crumble at my seeming aggression and this caused his smaller companion to fall back in his seat as well. There were a few grumbles from other customers around me. I started to remonstrate with them that this was my wife they were courting and a few more grumbles came from around me.

This set my wife off and she jumped up from her seat, smashed the top off a pint glass and brandishing it at me advanced upon me. I did not doubt that she would push it into my face without even blinking and the pub had a reputation for violence so the other customers may well have joined in. I kept my cool however and said, "Well, I have all the evidence I need now so you are wasting your time getting angry." I then moved towards the door and slowly left the bar hoping my show of bravado gave them pause for thought. It seemed to work and when I got outside I smartly left the area keeping a wary eye on the pub door. Thankfully no one came out to find me.

It took some time to convince my Solicitor to get my case into court and he seemed to make excuses to send me letters and slow things down as much as he could. I did not realise at that point that each and every letter was a cost against me. I had already established that I had no financial obligation to this woman so it seemed more than possible that no order against me to pay any money out would be made. I therefore, in hindsight, believe that it was entirely probable that the Solicitor was trying to increase my costs to cover any loss he had by not having to process my payments through his books, for which I presume he would have charged a percentage.

In the meantime I had started a relationship with my Sister's friend Pat and when the divorce absolute date came through we set the date for my second wedding.

# Foreign Affairs

At first on entering my second marriage I felt confident that my Wife was intelligent and able to control our finances as well as we required. She initially seemed to confirm this by going to the extent of shopping in several supermarkets each week and only buying the loss leaders in each store. These were goods that were priced low and advertised in order to lure in the customers who would then spend a fortune buying their weekly shop because it was convenient being in the shop where the goods were on display. This way the store might lose a little on a few items but would more than make up for it by the profits they made on normally priced items. Having purchased these items my Wife would have surveyed the prices of other items in each shop and would then purchase the cheapest available items for our other weekly needs. In this and in other ways my Wife seemed to be level headed and frugal with our money earned, which all went into one joint account.

However, when we had our two children she seemed to change and stop heeding the bank statements which I trusted her to open and deal with accordingly. As a Self Employed Engineer I would keep accounts and pay my tax and insurances once a year against my accounts which were submitted and agreed by the Inland Revenue. According to the Inland Revenue my agreed accounts for nineteen seventy nine dictated that I pay an amount of tax that I, in my innocence, supposed would be in the bank.

Unfortunately the money was not there because my wife had spent it. According to my rate of earning and the amount we required to live each month there should have been more than enough to pay this bill with an excess left in our account for a rainy day.

Needless to say I was very surprised and deeply disappointed. Having apologised to the Inland Revenue, I decided that to stay in England and incur more tax liability whilst I tried to pay off what I owed would be somewhat counter- productive.

I discussed the situation with my Family and decided it would be more efficient if I went to work abroad where I could earn more than I could in England and not incur any tax liability as long as I stayed for at least one year. I had spent one month in Saudi Arabia sorting out problems on a previous contract redesigning all the electrics on the new Jeddah Airport on behalf of an English consultancy. This made me feel comfortable and confidant in going back and being able to cope. I managed to get a contract in Saudi Arabia which was to be open ended so reluctantly off I went.

The Manager of my new employers told me I had to wear two hats. One hat was that of Senior Supervising Engineer and (Because of my training in psychology from my hobby)the second hat was Personnel Manager for the Thai Engineers who were employed by the company. I proceeded to carry out my duties in my usual diligent manner and discovered the Thai's were not paid sufficient food allowance monies each month. The net result of this was that they had to go fishing off the beach regularly in order not to starve. Their appetites like themselves were not big so they did not overspend on food, in fact they paid from their own pockets, one day a week, to eat out at a restaurant that specialised in Thai cuisine. This was one way to reduce the strain on their food allowance but there was still insufficient monies for their needs. There were other problems such as a non-air conditioned twelve seat bus to travel sixty miles each way to work every day, and to sometimes use during the day, this being in and through a desert country.

Saudi Arabia. 1980.

They were called 'Third World Citizens' and were treated in a less than third class way in all aspects. This was made even more unfair because they were expected, and did with a smile on their faces, to work much harder than most of their co-worker's from other areas of the world.

One day one of them sat at his drawing board refusing to work and throwing a very sharp knife repeatedly into his drawing board. No person would go near him because the other Thai's assured us that he had been involved in knife fights in Bangkok and would not hesitate to use it. I tried speaking to him but he would not answer. His colleagues told me a mistake had been made in the main office and he had not received his salary. Instead of coming to me with his problem he had gone straight to the 'In Country' Manager. The Manager had said too bad, promised to inform the main office next time he spoke to them and that it would be paid the next month. In the meantime he would have to wait until then to get his money. The Thai allowed me to approach him and I told him he should have come to me first but I would go to the manager and speak with him. The Brit's in the office expressed surprise that he accepted me and the other Thai's, who would not approach him themselves, said, "It is okay Derek is our friend."

When I spoke to the manager he was intransigent and also asked why I got involved. I reminded him of my two titles and he said, "Don't be daft you are not supposed to do any personnel work that's only a titular position to keep the Arab's happy." I promised to discuss my position later but explained the Thai's position. They had told me that he had to send the money home regularly to pay for essential medical treatment for a relative who would die without it, so he could not wait until the next month.

I suggested that we could use the petty cash to pay for the treatment and he would repay it next month. The Manager said the whole of the petty cash was accounted for by essential equipment and he was not prepared to jeopardise the company position. I then suggested we have a whip round to raise the necessary cash, again he refused on the grounds that nobody, including me, had the time to waste. When he emphasised the, 'including you,' bit I realised he was quite upset that I had been doing the job I had been given.

I went back to the Thai and told him we were going to raise the cash he required and he would have to give it back to me at the end of the month so that I could repay it, so would he please give me the knife to dispose of and return to his work. He said to me, "If Manager keep telling me to get back to work and he stand where you are, I stick him, if he stand by door, I throw knife." As he said those words he threw the knife and it stuck in the door jam. He then said, "I aim good, see."

He followed this with tears springing to his eyes and he cuddled me and said thank you. Later I was informed by his colleagues that the relative was his daughter who had extremely bad kidney problems. Whilst sending money home I was able to keep some money with me in order to save and buy presents for my family to take on leave with me. Fortunately I had enough to give to the Thai to send home and pay for his daughter's vital treatment, which I did the following day without telling him where the money came from.

It is probably as well to explain the pay structure that seemed to exist in Arab countries at that time, as I understood it. Amongst a number of men doing the same job, at the same level, in the same company, the Arab would get a level of pay we can describe as one hundred per-cent. An American would get about ninety five per-cent, Europeans would get about sixty to seventy per-cent and third World country people would get about thirty three per-cent. This meant it was not too much to expect me to have sufficient funds to do what I did and the Thai paid me back immediately he had the funds. It was claimed that salaries were paid in accordance with cost of living rates in the different parts of the world and led to strange situations.

Our Technical Manager in that company was a Scottish man, quite young and holding a Higher National Certificate in Engineering. An American holding a Doctorate in Chemical Engineering and seventy years of age, came to work with us and under the Technical Manager. American qualifications were always rated below English Qualifications. The Doctor, working under the Scotsman, had a higher salary than his boss. The first thing the Doctor did was ask what the 'other lever' in the central consul of his company car was. He was told it was a gear shift and he said he had not seen one in his entire life. He stated that it would not be a problem and promptly reversed the car into a lighting column doing a great deal of damage to a car that had just a few delivery kilometres on the clock.

One of my fellow British Engineers on this contract seemed to take a dislike to me after two or three months for no apparent reason. Then one day one of the Thai's made mention, also for no apparent reason, to an intimate part of that Engineers anatomy. I had thought that the closeness between myself and the Thai's was because I was genuinely trying to help them on the personnel side of their contracts. It seemed the other Engineer had some other type of closeness to them and he was jealous because he mistook my friendship with the Thai's for something else. However this Engineer was noteworthy for some other reason.

The oil plant we were working on was at a place called Abquaiqu (pronounced abcake) and at that time it was said that Saudi Arabia was producing half the worlds supply of oil and that two thirds of that oil went through Abquaiqu during its processing. Indeed there was one pipe above ground which was large enough to drive a four wheel drive vehicle through with room to spare. If you stood next to this pipe you could feel the ground trembling with the oil rushing through twenty four hours a day. There were also two oil flares at the plant, sometimes both running but mostly only one. These very impressive flares could be seen from a great distance because they were both one hundred and fifty yards long and seventy feet high. These burnt off the excessive gas that was a bye product of the oil plant processing.

This is the story as I heard it from Engineers on site.

Health and safety at the plant had become lax and some vehicles that were not given clearance to enter the plant had been allowed to enter. At the end of a shift on the day in question a car full of workers was being followed off site by a coach and the car went through a pocket of gas and the engine stopped. The driver, not thinking, tried to restart the engine and the extra power needed to start the engine produced a spark large enough to ignite the gas and the resulting explosion apparently destroyed not only the car and its occupants but also the coach and its occupants behind it.

This incident had started a fire destroying most of the plant and because it was so important it had been rebuilt in a great hurry, no doubt with a few updating modifications, but it had been made to do its job as fast as possible. Because of this there were no updated drawings of the plant and all its instrumentation and we were employed to survey all the relevant plant and produce the required instrumentation drawings for future maintenance and repair work. There were also a large number of outlying plants, some many kilometres away and the record drawings for these, being stored at the main plant, were destroyed in the fire. These were Gas and Oil separation plants (GOSPS for short). The company would give us Supervising Engineers a map, some old drawings, a compass and a four wheel drive vehicle, tell us to pick a team of Thai Engineers and go out and find the GOSPS to survey them and update the drawings. The indication of where to find the plants was the pointing of a finger almost randomly at the map and we had to find the right co-ordinates to find the plant. The rules we were given when going out into the desert were as follows;

Take five gallons of water per person per day plus an extra five gallons.

If your vehicle broke down or got stuck in the sand, stay with your vehicle because it was easier to spot than an individual and it afforded you some shade at the height of the day when the sun was at its hottest.

Always wear a hat and shirt with long sleeves to protect your arms when in the desert sun.

Remember that, because of the brightness of the sun, when in the desert you could often see things that were a long distance away and you got the impression that they were a lot closer than they actually were.

This other Engineer had been given a map and the other items plus the order to go out and find a GOSP.. When he left the office he took one gallon of water to serve himself and two Thai Engineers and he had no hat, even a hard hat for use on the plant. Their vehicle got stuck in the sand in the desert. The Engineer looked around and spotted an oil plant in the distance. Because he could see it he told his Thai's they were close and they were going to walk to the plant to get help.

According to the Thai's,' when I spoke to them, they said he removed his shirt, revealing his bare body to the sun. He then took of his shoes. This he felt made him keep moving his feet because the sand was so hot he had to keep lifting his feet and consequently would not be able to stop walking.

The Thais, not understanding, followed suit because he was the boss and must know best what to do. The plant they could see was in fact fifteen miles from their vehicle and that distance at midday was a killer. Luckily when they were near exhaustion and still a long way from the plant, someone was working at the top of a piece of very high plant called a, Catalytic Cracker. This person looked out to the desert, saw them and raised the alarm. A vehicle was sent out to bring them in and they were saved from what may well have been their deaths.

This British Engineer was an aggressive, argumentative individual and trouble in the making. In spite of that and this problem he had made worse by his ignorance, the company was so greedy for profit that instead of dismissing him and returning him to England they gave him a slight reprimand, which he just shrugged off, and sent him back to work.

On oil plants there are always gas pockets building up so stringent measures like no smoking were applied very vigorously and yet on more than one occasion I turned a corner and found third world country workers sitting on oil pipes smoking instead of working. Among them on one occasion was this same British Engineer.

It seems that on overseas contract work of this type there are always interesting things happening. It was during this particular contract in nineteen eighty that the Aramco main contract came to an end and the Americans who had been managing the whole of the Saudi oil industry lost their managerial position. The net result of this was that the Saudi's took over the management of the whole company.

At this time a friend I had made who always acted as my Snooker and Pool partner was given a new job and a rise in status and suddenly seemed to disappear. His name was Dave and he was an ex London policeman who was working as a security advisor for Aramco. A couple of months later I was walking across the plant to go and play Bridge at the house of a Lebanese couple I had also befriended. I heard someone call my name and there was Dave walking towards me. I greeted him warmly and asked where he had been. He said his new job meant that once a month he had to take a quantity of alcoholic beverage to the house of the local Police Chief. He was then made to sit with the police chief and consume a whole bottle of Whisky with him for the rest of the evening. If Dave had been caught with this consignment on his truck he would of course have been on his own to face the consequences. However he had something interesting to show me but I must not leave his side for fear that I would get shot. He took me to what he referred to as a block house and inside were six American soldiers in uniform. Standing around the block house were many Saudis armed with so many guns and bands of ammunition and knives that it was a wonder they were able to keep on their feet. He greeted them all at once and pointed to me and said loudly, "Ana sideek," which meant this is my friend. He explained that I could now safely walk away as long as it was not towards the block house. He then explained that some Bedouwins had reported seeing the soldiers photographing an oil installation in the desert and Dave had been sent out in charge of these Saudi soldiers to bring the Americans in for questioning. It was illegal to photograph oil installations and apparently these men had been sent in covertly to obtain the information the Americans had discovered they had not taken with them when they were kicked out by the Saudis.

On another occasion before Dave had been promoted, he had walked into the recreation hall one night, greeted me loudly and slammed a clipboard down very pointedly on a table and looking at me nodded towards it and said, "I am getting myself a cake and a drink from the fridge." I walked over as if to shake his hand and read a letter on the clip board. The letter was from the local police chief telling Dave officially that the Police were to raid the camp that night to try and find a Filipino who was wanted for alcohol related crimes.

I made sure every person there knew and the place emptied immediately so that people could hide their illegal drink and warn their friends to do the same. Dave explained that three Filipinos had been discovered brewing illegal Sideeky (an alcoholic drink) in the desert and two had been caught but the third had stabbed a policeman and escaped.

We were in what was said to be the smallest Construction camp in Saudi Arabia and yet there were five thousand inhabitants. The place was apparently more alive that night than it normally was during the day, some people climbed the fence and took their booze and buried it in the desert, some wriggled under the living quarters and buried their booze there and one poor American individual had come face to face with a Scorpion under there.

Apparently he just froze and screamed and started crying so someone just unceremoniously dragged him out not knowing what was happening to him. The Scorpion apparently ignored him but he got very boring and spent much time interrupting our Snooker and Pool games telling us about his great adventure that scared him half to death.

The company who ran the camp for Aramco were called Saudi Catering and on one occasion decided to do something for some charity or other. They decided to get people to team up and swim a relay race of one hundred lengths of the pool. Sitting close to us at the time of the announcement was an American who attached himself to us and somehow by talking nonstop made himself our team Captain. We could not have cared less and let him do it as long as we were participating in some way. Tactics were discussed and we decide to meet the next week and practice. It turned out our 'Captain' who was about six feet, six inches tall could only swim a maximum of two strokes before he started to sink and swallow copious amounts of water and he came up coughing and spluttering. My other companions had imbibed a little alcohol and didn't care so I just went along with it for the laugh. In the event we did participate and in spite of our Captain we came fifth and each received the appropriate certificate.

The company had an office in a place called Al Khobar and one day one of our Managers was going out to attend a meeting. The office was on a dual carriage way and when he went out carefully driving on the correct side of the road, a Saudi suddenly turned a corner in front of him driving the wrong way on the road and hit him head on. The Saudis were notorious for this sort of thing and as it was a dual carriage way it was obvious who was in the wrong. Our man said, "Right I've got you bang to rights," and went to find a policeman. When he returned with a policeman he was surprised to find the cars were now facing in the opposite direction. He was arrested and we spent a month visiting him in prison to feed him some food, that he found edible, every day.

We were discussing this one evening and asking if there was a way our colleague could prove his innocents. One of the other Managers said it was impossible and backed up his comment with the following story. In a court case that the company had been involved with some time before, an employee of the company had gone to a meeting on the companies behalf and had parked his car correctly in the correct allocated place in the road. A Saudi driver had come along in his car and had hit the parked car doing a great deal of damage.

The Judges ruling was that it was the fault of the driver who was correctly parked and no where near the scene at the time of the crash. His justification was that if the foreign driver had not accepted the contract to work in the country he would not have gone to the meeting and consequently would not have parked the car where it was so if the car was not there the crash could not have happened. Our informant said the company had paid a lot of money in compensation and would never forget it.

Markets in Arab countries are called 'Souks' and there is always something going on. On one occasion in the souk I was leaving a gold shop and turned to look into a window at something I had not noticed before. As I turned away I bumped into a very large man in military garb and my face was at the level of his upper chest. When I looked up Idi Armin was smiling at me and I apologised and hurried away glancing fearfully at his two even bigger bodyguards.

A number of the gold shops were very small and compact and on one occasion I stood back from the counter to let an Arab lady pass but instead of passing she started to look at items in the glass topped counter. She was a large lady dressed all in black as usual and had to bend to see closely the merchandise. In so doing she pressed her rear up against me and trapped me against a showcase behind me, she was giggling at her companion and kept moving slightly so that she rubbed up against me.

On another occasion, at Abquaiqu A man came running up to me and said, "Sideek, sideek you first aid." I said. "Yes." and he said, "Please sideek, come quick accident." I naturally went to see if I could help and got what some would call a big surprise. He took me to the rough road that ran through the souk and indicated a body on the ground that was covered with a sheet. He gesticulated at the truck and said, "Hit, Hit." so I went to the body wondering why they had covered it completely with the sheet.

When I pulled the sheet back the body was headless and in a sort of stupor I asked where the head was and the man indicated a lump, also covered, in the darkness looking like a football at the side of the road some distance away. Whilst thinking, *no blood so he must have died instantly,* I suddenly thought, oh no I'm here to be the fall guy, so I stood up and ran so fast even Yusain Bolt could not have caught me.

I reiterate what I said previously, there are always incidents happening when on contract in foreign climes. I have a T-shirt with the logo on it which says, 'I survived the abquaiqu Highway' and if you really survived the Abquaiqu Highway, as I did for fifteen months, you had almost created a miracle. There were two notable car related incidents that I witnessed personally on this road.

One day we were just leaving Al Khobar to go to our office in Abquaiqu and we were stopped at a traffic light. An American saloon car pulled up beside us and there were two or three men in the front and several muslim women in the back. Sitting on laps and playing on the floor were a number of children. We noticed them more because they pulled up very fast and so close to our car that we were hoping they would not hit us as they pulled away from the lights. Comments were made about how many people they managed to cram into a car. In keeping with the speed they had been going when they approached the traffic signal, as the lights changed they accelerated away very fast. When we had gone a short distance along the desert road we came across the car once again.

In Saudi Arabia there are many large lorries that are lit by many lights all over so that they tend to be very noticeable. They are also quite high off the ground, so high in fact that the bonnet (hood to an American) of a saloon car will just go beneath the back of the lorry. At the point in the road where we again came across this vehicle there was a cross road which was very difficult to see. The vehicle had obviously been travelling at high speed and had collided with one of these lorries (trucks to an American) that had been traversing the crossing. The car had hit the midpoint of the truck and was stuck almost completely out the other side. The top of the car was totally sheered off and I think every adult was beheaded but the children were writhing about in the bottom of the vehicle covered in blood and gore from the adults bodies. Having looked our driver cursed and accelerated away because he knew that if any foreigner was present at such an incident the locals would try every trick in the book to lay the blame on their doorstep.

The second incident I witnessed, again on the same notorious 'Abquaiqu Highway', involved a beautiful white Cadillac. We were again on our way to the office when this Cadillac passed us at high speed. We saw it going into the distance and it passed what looked like a low loader truck with a large squarish load. The car had about five well dressed Arab men on board. At the side of the road there was only one large layby with no facilities but lots of space for vehicles to park. One of our passengers wanted to stop and urinate so we decided the layby was the only safe place on such a dangerous road.

As we entered the area we saw the low loader entering in front of us and realised its load was a large oblong, very heavy electric transformer. The Cadillac was parked up with its occupants still inside. The desert roads in Saudi are not the best and strongest and yet they seem to last sometimes many years carrying many large loads. Although I have seen large sections of road that had lifted in heavy rain and aquaplaned across the desert on flood water.

In this incident, as the low loader was passing the Cadillac the road gave way at one point and the low loader tipped sideways and the load slipped off onto the car. It seemed to happen in slow motion like in a film for maximum impact. The load on the truck was so heavy it had not been fastened down and even if it was any fastening would never hold under such circumstances.

Three of the car tyres popped out sideways and the other must have buried itself in the surface. The car and its occupants ended up looking about six to nine inches high. The top of the vehicle apparently was as flat as the side of the transformer that squashed it. We were told that the car was taken and buried, as it was, in the desert because the occupants could not possibly be removed from the wreck that remained.

On another occasion I was driving a four wheel drive vehicle with some Thai Engineers and for a change we had found a road which took us generally in the direction we needed to go.

The road we were on was a dual carriage way with a central reservation wide enough to accommodate one of the big trucks, two lanes in each direction and a wide hard shoulder each side of the road. We noticed a large load coming towards us from the opposite direction. It was not unusual to see a thirty foot by thirty foot temporary office on the back of a large Kenilworth truck being transported together with a couple of very large tanks from one place to another. We were prepared to drive very close to or maybe even on the hard shoulder, depending upon the driving skills of the oncoming driver.

In this case it had all those elements plus lots of pipework and several bits of heavy equipment on a number of trucks. Also, leading the convoy, was an oil exploration drilling rig. The wheels on the rig towered over our four wheel drive and the load was so wide it's wheels were only just on the outer edges of the hard shoulder and threatening to slip of either side. We were forced out onto the soft sand at the side of the road and even so we were still under parts of the rig as we passed. I had seen sets of wheels, of the same size as those on the rig, being transported on big trucks, previously and wondered where the Saudi's were building jet airliners. I also later saw a thirty foot wide steel ball, which was a pressure vessel, on those same size wheels, and it had a Toyota truck parked underneath it where an engineer was checking the wheels had been fitted safely to the underside to take it on its journey to a new site.

Yet another happening was on my first day of arrival when I was being introduced to the other residents of a villa that we were due to stay in initially. One man who entered the room was very tall and very thin, which must have increased the illusion of height. He also wore a cowboy style hat with an Ostrich feather sticking out of the hat band. When he first saw me he smiled but on hearing my name his face dropped and he hurriedly made an excuse and left the room. One or two people including myself expressed astonishment at his behaviour and I was informed that he was normally very agreeable and his personality made the others like him.

This mans job entailed supervising trench digging and cable laying which meant he was in a different department to myself. I did not meet him again until the following night when he returned from the daily grind. Everybody was going to have a drink of the illegal liquor that they had purchased from where ever. Whilst they were getting organised unearthing well hidden bottles etc. I tackled him about his seeming problem with me as I did not want any bad atmosphere to arise and spoil what looked like a promising situation.

He told me I was already aware of his problem and that he would prefer I got on with it and did the job I had really come to do. I of course was mystified and he asked me if I knew a certain gentleman from an Essex town. I said remarkably I did know the gentleman concerned, he was my Uncle but I had only heard of him and nearly met him about twenty years before when circumstances prevented our meeting. My Father had said he was his step Brother and not really a person I should mix with so I did not pursue it and had nearly forgotten his existence. I did not say this bit but just admitted to knowing of him.

He insisted that I had been told about him and the amount of money he owed my Uncle and that my Uncle had sent me out to kill him for it. I of course denied this and assured him I was only out there to earn some much needed cash so that I could get back to my family.

He of course assumed that I would be paid a lot by my Uncle and that was the cash I was after. I could only assure him and get on with my proper work. He however never lost the conviction of what my real task was and persisted on worrying about me and what skills I must have in order to do it. One day he was so drunk he could hardly move, let alone stand up, and the man who's room we were in wanted to go to bed. I volunteered to help him up the stairs to his room and dump him on his bed so he could sleep it off and the other man could get some badly needed sleep.

We were approaching the top of a staircase with my right hand behind his back and his arm over my shoulder being held by my left hand when he suddenly swung his fist round as hard as he could and punched me in the stomach. My stomach muscles were taught with supporting his weight and his punch was like a small child tapping me to get my attention.

I remonstrated with him and said I was only helping him and he said, "Get it over with, kill me now, then you can go home to your family." I said if that was what I wanted I could have done it many times and in many ways and the fact that I had not must surely be proof of my non intention to harm him. He persisted however and told me when I left the country that he expected me back to do the job.

Although I was entitled to three weeks holiday every three months I only came home twice in the fifteen months I worked on this contract because I was paid the fare and travelling expenses whether I came home or not. I also got paid a little extra for working during that time so it was worthwhile because it meant I was getting more cash for the whole trip.

My board and lodgings were free for the whole tour and I was able to send home one thousand pounds per month and keep at least three hundred pounds per month in my pocket, which I used to buy presents for my family, and the rest I saved.

My second wife had assured me she had learnt her lesson so, like a fool I trusted her. She only needed Two hundred and fifty pounds per month to live so I expected a nice amount of savings to be waiting for me on my return. My wife knew How much I owed the tax man and I felt assured that, with my savings, I had plenty of time to settle into a new job.

Unfortunately this gave my second wife time to shoot herself in the foot and ruin our lives forever. She insisted that my children write to me regularly and keep me up with their progress and growing up whilst I was away. This they did religiously and in the process told me often about 'Uncle Paul'. I did not have any idea who this person was but being told by my children how he took them out very often with their Mother it did not take much of a leap of logical thinking to realise their Mother was having an affair. I came back to England as fast as I could. When I got home I faced my Wife with the whole story and she, in spite of being fully aware of my reason for going overseas and the fact that her rash spending had been the main motivating force. In spite of the fact that my efforts were all in the hopes of keeping our marriage alive and assuring our future. She came out with the weakest excuse she could have thought up and said she thought that I had left her and she thought she was in love with this man.

This totally ignored the fact that there was barely two thousand pounds left in my account out of the fifteen thousand I sent. This meant that she had been using my money to finance this whole affair and all my efforts had come to nothing. What also rubbed salt into the wound was that the man was the brother of my Sister's so called other best friend so my sister must have known what was going on but never even hinted of it. This meant that my sister must have colluded with my wife because they had been best friends when I met my wife and my sister had proved that, for her, blood was not thicker than water. Indeed, facts that I later found out about my sister and her relationship with her second Husband pointed in the direction of her doing something similar to my second wife's behaviour to me, to her first Husband.

I next went to Saudi Arabia as a result of the recession in nineteen ninety three, this time to Jeddah. In England I had been put out of work by circumstances beyond my control (See Hypno Centre Travesty) and needed to find some way of earning money. I admit I cheated because the Government at that time allowed an individual to attend what was called a job club once per week to seek work but I was attending two job clubs. One in the new forest and one in London and I was sending out twelve job applications per day for many weeks. During this time, also according to the law, the Government should have been paying the interest on my mortgage. This also went wrong as usual whilst I was an innocent party (See Illegal repossession). Eventually I was offered a position in Saudi Arabia which I felt I was unable to refuse. I decided to accept the job which would make me no longer a liability to the state and give me a chance to get back on the straight and narrow.

The position required me to design fire alarm systems (to detect, to sound the alarm and fight fires.) in power plants around Jedah in Saudi Arabia. Having spent a month there some years before I felt a certain familiarity with the area and quite confident that I could cope.

Our office in Jeddah was on an open area between two sites owned by others. One day the owner of one of these sites decided to start building an office block. They dug down about fifteen feet, a large hole and before they got to their required depth they were digging under water because Jeddah is on the red sea coast and they were below sea level.

There was a fence erected between the site and the road and a large metal sign erected on two metal posts. With the excavation being in sand and the bottom of the hole from about eight feet down being full of water it was inevitable what would happen.

The sides of the hole started to fall into the water and after one day the large metal sign fell into the water, about two days later the fence started to go the same way. After this the hole crept towards the road and the pavement started to disintegrate. In the meantime the contractors were filling the hole with large rocks.

The hole meanwhile was also creeping towards our building and I watched with trepidation waiting for the day that we were told to evacuate. Some of the services to our building started to appear as the hole crept closer and they had to be supported in order that they remain doing their job for us. Eventually the rocks were high enough for them to put down a layer of concrete and when it finally set they started to install reinforcing irons which meant we could heave a sigh of relief and relax as they started to overcome the subsidence possibility.

One of the plants we were working on was in Mecca so we required a special letter from the king in order to be allowed to enter the edge of the town. We were never allowed to go further in because we were not Muslims. We were told we could not take photographs because of things like a beautiful mosque that was next to the plant we were working on.

Unfortunately that was the spur some people needed to find excuses to take pictures of our work 'for record purposes' and 'to show our progress'. So a pile of spoil (useless soil) taken out of the ground accidentally contained views of the mosque. When travelling to Mecca during Ramadan I felt sure I had seen a large mound of some sort appear out in the desert too far to actually discern what it was. When I questioned one or two people about it I was told two main stories, one was that it was a pile of sheep bodies that had been sacrificed and piled there to dispose of them. After all, each male who attends to view and pray at 'The Cabbah', apparently has to sacrifice a sheep to Allah. The other story denied this and claimed that a refridgerated ship was requisitioned to take the sheep bodies to some African country and distribute them to the starving poor. I never discovered the real answer to my question so either one could be true.

Of course there are good and bad people in every walk of life and the person I am about to report on may not even be a Muslim. During Ramadan this man came into our Jeddah office with a young girl child on his arm and holding her arm as if to ensure she was safe and would not fall off. He told us a story that he had saved for many years to come to Mecca and bring his family. He said while he was there someone stole all his money and papers so he had no return ticket to take his family home and no food or anywhere to stay. As he said this he visibly squeezed the child's arm very severely so that the child cried. This gave him cause to say, "See my child is so hungry she is always crying for food and I need to feed the whole family."

Apparently these children are for rent and many people hire them from their parents in order to beg. It appears that it can be a very lucrative business in some countries.

When working on the Mecca plant I had to go through cable tunnels to find new cable routes for the fire alarm cables. These tunnels consisted of deep trenches with concrete sides and steel plates covering them. The plates were at least one inch thick because of much heavy traffic that was often used on the plants. I noticed that when in the tunnels I was always soaking wet but as soon as I left a tunnel I became stone dry. When a tunnel had had the plate removed so we could gain access I tried standing half in and half out of the tunnel and found that it was instant. When half in, the half outside was totally dry and the part inside was very wet and when I reversed my position the two sides of my body were instantly changed to the other condition. The sun bearing down and heating those plates made me think you could cook a roasting joint down there.

I made yet another enemy in this office. This man's name was Steve he was in his twenties, about a foot taller than me and managed to be always drunk outside of working hours. He and another man named Allen were living in the same villa as myself and we decided to take turns in cooking. One day when it was Steve's turn the next day he said I will cook you a beautiful steak tomorrow. We anticipated this occasion because he said he cooked his steaks in a certain way that was always successful and very tasty. When we arrived home the following day Allen and I were starving but Steve was not in evidence. Allen said, "Either he has got held up on site or he is shopping for some special ingredient."

In the event Steve arrived about one hour later and had forgotten he was cooking because he had been drinking with someone else. We reminded him and from looking confused he said I have not forgotten don't worry. He went to the oven and opened the door. As he opened it he stepped back quickly and we became aware of a horrendous smell. That morning when we left for work Steve had taken the steaks from the freezer and placed them in the unlit oven to thaw out all day. We could not believe it and informed him he should have put them in the fridge, especially in such a hot country. Allen had changed into his Pyjamas because he intended to stay in and read and listen to some music in his room. The only option open to us now was to go out to eat and we would have to wait for Allen to change back into outdoor clothes. We were starving hungry at this point and I am afraid I lost my temper at this idiocy which occurred because Steve was a drunk. I verbally attacked Steve and he just stood and stared blankly at me. Allen was afraid of upsetting Steve and said nothing but I was not putting up with the possibility of a regular occurrence of this type.

My decision regarding this was to tell Steve that, on top of the near misses we had suffered in cars because of his drunken behaviour, this was unacceptable, and he had to leave the villa and find a bed elsewhere.

Because of his height Steve had managed to commandeer the best car in the car pool and his threatening stance meant he kept the keys on his person. However on several occasions Steve, in a drunken state, had tried to drive straight across roundabouts and left his car in such a bad condition that it would have been written off in Britain. In Saudi however the mechanics worked hard on it and put it back on the road each time. Finally the company gave him an ultimatum and told him if he crashed the car one more time he would be dismissed. In the meantime everyone tried to carry on as normal and one day Allan had decided he would have a drink for his birthday and invited everyone to a party in our villa.

Because he had included everyone Steve turned up bringing his own music machine and with his Scottish drinking companion. I had no problem with his companion who was a good guy even when in his cups.

I was unsure of the outcome in regard to Steve however and kept a wary eye on him all evening. We had large double walled drink containers that held two or three litres of drink, had a spout and a pump so that you did not have to open the lid and let in air that could either cool or heat up the contents. I was sitting on the end of a large three seat settee and Steve was sitting on the other end. Steve was a coward when sober but, like many drunks, reckless when inebriated.

Having consumed the entire contents of his drink container and being drunk he suddenly lifted the container in the air and hurled it full strength at my head. I had been keeping an eye on him as I said and was able to move back a little and the container made a very large hole in the wall next to me. I immediately stood up and ordered Steve out of the villa. He in turn stood up and came towards me but his friend stood up also, positioned himself between us, and told Steve to calm down and suggested he do as I had demanded. Steve argued and I replied and was adamant that he should leave. I grabbed Steve's music centre, held it out at arms length and told him to take it with him because if he did not I would drop it on the concrete floor between us.

Steve leant forward in his usual threatening manner and said to me, "Before I leave this country I am going to kill you." I replied, "Bring it on Steve." I showed no fear of him and this made him hesitate and step back. I said, "Don't forget your Music", still holding it at arms length. He grabbed at it, turned and left. Nobody in that room knew how frightened I was and I was always shown respect thereafter.

Steve inevitably crashed the car again and was sacked. The car he drove was a two litre Mazda and was a beautiful car to drive at first so good and fast someone nicknamed it the Mazdarati. I drove the car one day when Steve was busy in the office and no other vehicle was available and it was a joy to use. I drove it later after Steve left and it was absolutely hell to drive, noisy when running, pulling over to one side and making a clicking sound and did not change gear easily at all.

A couple of months later the company folded and every employee was dismissed. I was owed some money and went to the villa that the country manager, who had misused the company funds which caused the company to fold, was living in. There had been rumours that he was involved in producing and selling illegal alcohol and when I got there, the evidence of this activity was not concealed. The Still they had set up was very sophisticated and I suspected that was where, at least some of, the company money had gone.

The ex-Company Manager just laughed at me and sitting among the men who surrounded him was Steve who had not left the country as dictated by the company after all. Being sober Steve just gloated and joined in the laughter but still did not have the guts to try and fulfil his promise to me. I am sure if he had and he had succeeded, his companions would have just taken my body out late at night and buried me in the desert to be gone without trace.

I was left with insufficient money to buy my ticket back to England but could do nothing about it. I had been made a friend of by a Saudi ten pin bowler at Jeddah bowling centre where I had met Osama Bin Laden. This Saudi friend told me about a scheme he had dreamed up to carry out in Cairo, Egypt. He asked my opinion and I highlighted what I thought he needed to do. He was over the moon because I had apparently echoed his thoughts as to what was required. He asked me to put something on paper for him and when I showed him graphically what I felt, he asked me to be his Managing Director and go to Egypt with him.

Having no other activity and the opportunity, it seemed, to start earning money again I said yes. Ali paid my fare and arranged everything so, leaving one or two items behind in his house for his wife to look after for me, we made our way by plane to Cairo. In Cairo we stayed at the Hilton for a day or two while we found an office to rent and I was introduced to Rushdi the man who was to become my assistant. The office had an apartment attached and I moved in temporarily while we furnished and set up the office sytems.

From this position Ali travelled about trying to find the first site to build what he wanted and I started to draw plans for the construction of a Sports Club which is a speciality of the Egyptian way of life. This club was to be able to hold international as well as national tournaments in different sports.

We were to include football, a gymnasium, ten pin bowling, track sports, tennis courts, Squash courts and table tennis etc. plus we were to include living accommodation for visiting athletes. In our original deliberations we agreed that ten pin bowling would be the first building to be made available together with some basic living accommodation for a skeleton staff to run and provide security as well as the facility. Whist this was happening initially Ali went backwards and forwards to and from Egypt and Saudi keeping in touch with his family and other activities that he was involved with.

In my efforts to make this company successful, I was prepared to accept any work that would lead to a cash flow, hopefully profitably.

When concentrating on the bowling alley aspect of the design of the sports club, I naturally made contact with a specialist manufacturer. One day they rang me and asked me to liaise with a hotel owner, in Cairo, who had a hotel in Sharm-El-Sheik. He wanted someone to go to his hotel and, survey to approve, a bowling alley he had built there.

We agreed that he would pay my fair for me to travel to England for Christmas, but I had to go via his hotel, carry out the survey, stay the night and then travel to England. On the return journey I was to go straight back to Cairo, having written and given my report when staying in Sharm-El-Sheik.

When I gave him the report, just before leaving for the airport, he read it quickly and laughed at me. Having noted some obvious movement in the side walls of the alley area, I had said, the pin setting area was too small and he should shut the building down and make that area bigger. He should then repair the damage at the top of two pillars in the middle of the side walls, to make them stronger and paint the new pin setting area with acoustic paint.

I stated that the noise from the pins being knocked down and then reset, was not only distracting for the players, but was affecting the main structure and would cause it to collapse.

I stated, that after this work, the larger area combined with the acoustic paint would make the sound, in the main alley area, much less and avert the current danger of collapse.

He called me stupid, saying, noise can not affect physical structures, but to enjoy my holiday. When I returned to Cairo, I went to his office and was informed he would not be available for a week, because he was not well. I said I hoped he would be better soon and could he phone me when he got back to report on what he had done with the bowling alley.

The receptionist then said it was the bowling alley that made him unwell. I naturally asked why and I was shown a picture of a beautiful young Egyptian girl.

I was then told that she was his niece, she had returned from Germany, for Christmas, because her employer had closed the business for the Christmas period until the new year. The family had gone to the hotel for the holiday period, in spite of being Muslim. She had been bowling when the roof collapsed and killed her.

A short while after this, my assistant Rushdie, told me he had heard the story that was being circulated about this incident. Apparently the hotel owner was saying, he had been shown a picture of his niece, taken in Germany. She was not wearing Muslim garb and was wearing a

skirt slightly above her knees, was showing her hair and had strong makeup on.

Apparently he was saying Allah had caused the collapse because she had become a bad Muslim.

Unfortunately each time Ali arrived at Cairo airport he purchased three or four bottles of whisky and contacted a friend of his who arranged for him to visit Casinos with various women who stayed with him night and day, and supplied him with various drugs. This it seems helped him to keep up with the demands of the women in bed and the night life when they could not be bothered with him. He also had to keep in touch with me and the various people we involved in our work.

It seemed he caught something nasty of one of his women and this led to his wife finding out about his activities. This led in turn to his wife saying to hell with the losses he was to make but banned him from coming to Cairo before we had spent a full year at our activities.

When Rushdi rang and asked him why we had not seen him for some while he explained and promised to send what he owed us and the company but that was the last we were to hear from him and we were left owed a great deal of money again. I had some extra design work to complete for a potential client but we were never paid for that either.

Again I was left without the ability to return to England so I set about getting work in Egypt. I was able to earn enough to live but not enough to come home to England.

I made some good friends in Cairo and one of them introduced me to my third wife. In nineteen ninety five my friend Val invited me to a St. Valentine's day party at her flat. Her Husband was to be home that day along with one or two other friends who normally worked away.

On the day Val introduced me to two Philippina ladies who were good friends of her also. After a while when I was in the kitchen topping up my drink Val came up to me and told me both ladies were single and available but she was saving one to introduce her to her Brother-in-Law. She did not tell me which one but having spent time with them I had a real good feeling about one of the ladies. There was one slim attractive but somewhat tired looking lady who it might be said, seemed to be approaching her sell by date. Her name was Gloria and it seemed she wanted me to be aggressive in my approach and she set me up for it by telling about two or three casual boyfriends she apparently had. The front runner it seemed was a commercial pilot employed by Egypt Air. In spite of his being the best person in her 'harem' she had time when he was away to see the others and enjoy their company.

The other lady was a warm approachable person who was very attractive, somewhat shy and retiring but an intelligent and independent person who appeared to be very kind but forthright and honest. She had a beautiful smile and impressed me very much.

Unlike Gloria, the other lady, Marsha, was not interested in impressing me but was still very friendly but not pushy. I was drawn to her almost immediately. At the end of the evening I had agreed to meet Marsha again and our relationship developed from there.

By June that year we moved in together and we married on January seventeenth, nineteen ninety six. I am extremely happy with our relationship and have no intention of letting it end if I have my way.

We stayed in Cairo until the year two thousand I had made some good friends in Egypt and was able to have some good times there. I had lost my property by this time and in spite of making enquiries during a holiday in nineteen ninety seven I had no luck in getting any compensation. The problem was that although I went into a government office to make the enquiries, I suffered from the usual 'government employee incompetence' and no record of my visit was made by them. This meant that when I made enquiries on my return to England in the year two thousand they informed me I had left too much time between approaching them. This was not true but I was left with no proof.

Of the friends I made in Cairo one was a Dental Surgeon, Egyptian born but with a British passport. He had worked in Harley Street for twenty five years and had the title 'Maxilo Facial surgeon'. He was a very good snooker and pool player and we played in the same pool team for a number of years. We were such good friends that he came to England on holiday after I returned, just so that we could play snooker together.

---

I had felt very strongly the loss of not knowing my Grandparents as a child and I was determined that my children would have as normal an upbringing as was possible and that their children would have the chance to know their Grandparents. I wanted to have a house big enough that at Christmas I could invite them all over to stay and enjoy a whole family Christmas together. With this in mind, in nineteen eighty one, I stayed with my wife, in spite of her being unfaithful, paid the taxman his money and changed my business to use what had been my hobby all my life so that I could start up a business near to my home. If I did not do this it meant that most of the time I had to work in London where most of the Engineering work I had been doing was available.

I even tried to employ my wife as my receptionist in this venture but she managed, by manipulating people, to use that against me. Unfortunately, because my wife had been unfaithful to me, I found it very difficult to respond to her in what should have been our intimate moments. I was able to succeed at first because I used my imagination to a great degree. When our intimate moments were down to one or two a month my wife found other activities for us and I was equally unhappy about those but by getting a bit of luck and using my ingenuity I was able to indulge once or twice. However my wife tried to manipulate the situation so that she could make it seem that the idea for these activities was mine I became even more anti and these activities stopped.

The net result of this was that my Wife started having another affair, this time with a man I had put myself out to help. His appreciation for my help was to start this affair with my wife which led to the final breakup of our marriage. Even under these circumstances, I refused to give my wife a divorce, because of my children, but she faced me with an ultimatum. Her words were, "I want all or nothing", and I was left with no alternative.

Whilst our divorce went through I even allowed my ex wife to stay in our bungalow because I could not put my youngest daughter out on the street. My daughter needed stability because she was fifteen and studying for important exams that were to have an influence on her future.

Believing that my ex wife's new lover was paying his own mortgage to keep his Mother from becoming homeless I allowed the couple to stay rent free in my bungalow for a year. In the meantime they were having a flat modified because they said his Mother would not allow my daughter in her house and was very nasty about it. Whilst all this was unfolding I had met and fallen for a beautiful young lady and we found a flat to live in temporarily in an old Water Mill which was still operating and used to vibrate as if an earthquake was happening when the water wheel ran. Whilst living in the mill I discovered that my ex's lover had not been paying his mortgage and had manipulated the situation so that he lost his property. Because of this he was able to put his own Mother into a home for the elderly that was run by the local council. This left him with no responsibility and free to do what he wanted.

This made me very angry that my ex and her lover had lived rent free for a year and had spent the time getting drunk and smoking, probably to my daughter's detriment, and generally living what I considered a debauched life without any apparent consideration for anyone else in the world.

Without guidance this situation led to my youngest daughter making some bad decisions in her life but thanks to her good sense she eventually made some very good decisions and made me as proud of her as possible to be. As I always felt would happen, her sister made good also and I am as proud of them both as much or more than any man could be.

Naturally my daughters do not wish to hear anything bad said about their Mother and I am made to stay silent. Unfortunately this situation has occurred too many times in my life and having to remain silent, leaves me feeling like I am yet again wrongly made to look a villain and be condemned by all and sundry. It is not just this situation but other scenarios, in which I was equally innocent, that existed at that time, contributed to this feeling of life's unfairness.

# Hypno Centre Travesty

## Preview

In 1980 at the end of March I returned from working for 15 months as an Engineer in Saudi Arabia. I had gone to work in Saudi Arabia to take advantage of the tax situation so that I could pay my taxes as a self - employed Engineer/Designer in England. This because my wife, at that time, had spent my money which was held back to pay my tax and insurance which the law insisted I pay. People may say that I was a fool to allow my wife access to my money at that time but she had been exemplary in looking after our finances when we had first got married in 1965 and I had at that point been able to trust her with all the family finances so I was somewhat misled into this situation.

My wife and I had discussed the situation in that it was impossible to earn the £2000 that I owed whilst working in England because as I earned the money so I gained more debt in tax and insurance which became payable to the government. We agreed that if I spent a year earning money abroad on which I would not incur tax but could pay the national insurance I would incur, we could maintain our marriage and our family which was precious to me.

I had felt very strongly the loss of not knowing my grandparents as a child and I was determined that my children would have as normal an upbringing as was possible and that their children would have the chance to know their grandparents. I wanted to have a house big enough that at Christmas I could invite them all over to stay and enjoy our whole family Christmas together.

With this thought in my mind I went to work in Saudi. Whilst I was in Saudi my wife insisted that my children keep in touch by letter so we retained the semblance of family. However my children sent me letters which mentioned 'Uncle Paul' who took them everywhere apparently. This filled me with suspicions about my Wife's behaviour. I returned in March 1981 and my wife admitted the affair trying to excuse herself by saying she thought I had left her and she thought she was in love with this man. These were just weak excuses because she knew that I had discussed with her the reasons for going to Saudi Arabia and the fact that I was coming back once the debt had been covered and our family life would resume. Apart from this we had met this man some years earlier at a party, he was the brother of my Sister's so called best friend at the time. I felt that this proved my previous suspicions to be correct. I decided that I would remain in England from then on in order to maintain my marriage especially for the sake of my children.

# The story after the history.

With this in mind, in 1981 I stayed with my wife in spite of her being unfaithful, paid the tax man his money and changed my business to use what had been my hobby all my life so that I could start up a business near to my home. If I did not do this it meant that a lot of the time I had to work in London where most of the engineering work I had been doing was available.

I may have mentioned previously, I had become interested in people and their behaviour when I was a child growing up in the Second World War. My family and I spent many hours in bomb shelters in the East End of London living through the Blitz and I spent these hours watching people reacting to the bombs falling and this made me extremely interested in them and their behaviour. Not only had this piqued my interest in people and their behaviour but it also had a big influence on how I shaped my own personality. This led me to begin my favourite hobby and spend much time people watching and studying various articles and documents on the subject of people.

Glady's, my best female friend. Circa 1963.

A friend that I had met through my wife to be had gone off to America to work in the 1960s and had rung telling me that she had read a book which she found very interesting. The reason for her interests she said was that every time she picked up the book to read it she kept getting a picture of me coming into her head because she said it explained my behaviour and my approach to life. When this friend returned to England she brought with her a copy of the book. She gave it to me so that I could read it and understand how she felt. Whilst I was reading the book this friend rang me in a very excited manner and said that the author was going to give a talk at the Savoy Hotel where he was based whilst he was in London on a visit. As I had started to get the same feelings that she did about this book, that this man had crawled into my head taken notes and came out and written it all down, I agreed to make enquiries as to the possibility of us going to visit this man on the occasion of his talk. When we arrived at the venue we were asked why we had requested to attend and repeated the reason I gave on the phone. When I gave my reasons I was asked if I would stay behind after the talk in order to have a word with the author of the book. When I spoke to the author, Dr Maxwell Maltz MD., FICS., he said he was very intrigued and asked if I would attend some special classes with the aim in mind of becoming what he called a 'workshop director' and teaching the principles of his book to other people as a means of 'self – improvement'.

Having agreed to this and having gone through the classes successfully, I then went around London and the South of England with a group of people where we gave talks to the public and formed a panel to answer questions on the subject after the meeting.

Part of my training had been to go through a workshop, merely as an experience, and after my training and during the time that we were giving our talks to recruit people to learn the system, I ran a number of successful workshops myself.

Having gone through this in the late 60s and having lost contact with the group because of work commitments in the interim, I carried on using the principles which were a natural part of my life anyway and now at the beginning of the 80s I decided to set up a practice to try to help people in their daily lives.

I even tried to employ my wife as my receptionist in this new venture but she managed, by manipulating people, to use that against me. Unfortunately, because my wife had been unfaithful to me, I found it very difficult to respond to her in what should have been our intimate moments. I was able to succeed at first because I used my imagination to a great degree. When our intimate moments were down to one or two a month my wife found other activities for us and I was equally unhappy about those but by getting a bit of luck and using my ingenuity I was able to indulge once or twice. However my wife tried to manipulate the situation so that she could make it seem that the idea for these activities was mine, I became even more anti-and these activities stopped.

The net result of this was that my wife started having another affair, this time with a man I had put myself out to help. His appreciation for my help was to start this affair with my wife which led to the final breakup of our marriage. Even under these circumstances I refused to give my wife a divorce, because of my children, but she faced me with an ultimatum. Her words were, "I want all or nothing", and I was left with no alternative. Whilst our divorce went through I even allowed my ex-wife to stay in our bungalow because I could not put my youngest daughter out on the street. My daughter needed stability because she was 15 and studying for important exams that were to have an influence on her future.

Believing that my ex-wife's new lover was paying his own mortgage to keep his mother from becoming homeless I allowed the couple to stay rent-free in my bungalow for a year. In the meantime they were having a flat modified because they said his mother would not allow my daughter in her house and was very nasty about it. Whilst all this was unfolding I had met and fallen for a beautiful young lady and we found a flat to live in temporarily in an old Watermill which was still operating and used to vibrate as if an earthquake was happening when the water wheel ran. Whilst living in the mill I discovered that my ex wife's lover had not been paying his mortgage and had manipulated the situation so that he lost his property. Because of this he was able to put his own mother into a home for the elderly that was run by the local council. This left him with no responsibility and free to do what he wanted. This made me very angry that my ex and her lover had lived rent-free for a year and had spent the time getting drunk and smoking, probably to my daughter's detriment, and generally living what I considered a debauched life without any apparent consideration for anyone else in the world.

My Wife and I had made a rule that my daughter must let us know exactly where she would be at any point in time whilst she was out of the house. There was to be no exception to this rule but we would only contact her in dire emergency so she would not feel hemmed in by our over attention and smothering behaviour. One evening it was very foggy and cold and I was to go out to play league snooker for my team. When I left the mill I was stopped very quickly by people with torches because a car with some village youngsters in it had crashed into a ditch. I tried making enquiries but could get no information about the occupants of the vehicle.

I decided to visit my Wife and her boy friend to ask where my Daughter was. When I arrived I was so anxious that I just put my key in the door and walked straight in. My Wife came out of the lounge in a dressing gown and her boy friend was lying on the floor covering himself and still watching the blue movie they had on. My Wife asked him to freeze frame it so she did not miss anything. I ignored this and explained about the accident and asked my Wife where my Daughter was.

She replied, "Isn't it great, the interest rate has gone down and the house is worth more money." I was absolutely surprised and repeated my request on the whereabouts of my Daughter. My Wife admitted she did not know and showed no concern whatsoever. I became angry and pointed out our Daughter could be lying in the ditch injured and that was the only important thing to consider. She could only make some other remark about house values and I angrily walked out to search the village for my Daughter. I eventually found her at the other end of the village and gave her a telling off about not informing her Mother where she was going. After ascertaining that she was alright I went on to my snooker game.

Without proper guidance this situation led to my youngest daughter making some bad decisions in her life but thanks to her good sense she eventually made some very good decisions and made me as proud of her as possible to be. As I always felt would happen, her sister made good also and I am as proud of them both as much or more than any man could be. Naturally my daughters do not wish to hear anything bad said about their mother and I am made to stay silent. Unfortunately this situation has occurred too many times in my life and having to remain silent, leaves me feeling that I'm yet again wrongly made to look a villain and be condemned by all and sundry. It is not just this situation but other scenarios, in which I was equally innocent that existed at that time, contributed to this feeling of life's unfairness.

As I said, I decided in March nineteen eighty one to set up my own business using what had been my hobby all my life in order to stay local to my home and use my knowledge and talents, such as they were, to help others. My knowledge of the 'Self- image' and how to use that knowledge for the benefit of others was to stand me in good stead. I took a course run by a professional institute on hypnosis and how to use it to help people who were struggling with life. To save time I will now reprint below an article I wrote a couple of years ago.

# 'SAD ', By Any Other Name

**Author : Derek Fairey**
16 - 07 -2010.

In the early to mid sixties I was introduced to a book called, 'Psycho-Cybernetics' by Maxwell Maltz MD FICS..

The introduction from a friend was, "You must read this book, every time I read it I get a picture of you." Whilst I was reading the book the person who recommended it to me rang me and told me that she had read in a London newspaper that Dr. Maltz was coming to London and would be giving a talk about the content of the book at London's Savoy Hotel. We decided to attend the talk if possible. I rang to book and was asked by the person taking my call why I wanted to go.

I explained my friends comment and my subsequent feeling whilst reading the book.

*As I read I felt as if this person had got into my head, made notes and then wrote down what he had discovered and published it.*

I was asked if I would introduce myself to Dr. Maltz at the talk. I did so and was invited to the Doctor's room at the Savoy hotel where he was staying. In the room he proceeded to question me, declared his amazement and requested that I attend a few lectures to learn how to present his work. I would then become a 'Workshop Director' and run workshops in self-improvement through the enhancement of the persons self- image.

As a result of this activity a group of us travelled mainly around London giving talks to attract people to the Workshops. We would take turns in giving the talk or sitting on a panel answering questions put by our audience after the talk.

These talks were the way we were advised to advertise what we were trying to do.

When enough people showed interest we would get them together to form a workshop. These workshops would meet at regular intervals and they would be given suitable set Information and interactive exercises which we directed. They were also given homework assignments which kept them active on a daily basis which was important for continuity.

When any one person disclosed a deep or more significant problem it was our job to deal with this either personally, but apart from the group, or by passing them on to a more qualified colleague.

Since my experiences as a child in London's bomb shelters during the second world war I had been interested in people and their reactions to situations. Now, given this opportunity, I started to read other related works in earnest.

In my chosen reading I came across references to sight and the rods and cones in the eye and their positions related to colour perception and the peripheries of vision. In Psycho-cybernetics individuals were advised to, "Hold your head up and face the world full on." Also there was a lot of reference to confidence. This confirmed my own conclusion that confidence or the lack of it was very important in people's lives and their achievements.

I had also observed that sometimes, in spite of not having suitable knowledge, people confidently went ahead in a venture and succeeded regardless.

In Psycho-cybernetics however we cautioned the need for realism in order to avoid the possible disasters that could occur with the subsequent devastation of a personality.

I noted that people with confidence problems looked down at the floor more often than anywhere else. They seemed to be looking at their feet as if they wanted to avoid walking into traps and problems or making eye contact with others. Eye contact with others often led to closer contact and more personal interaction which produced even more possible problems they would find difficulty in dealing with.

I also noted that such people were very often accident prone. On considering this I felt that the reason they were accident prone was that their lack of confidence led them to concentrate harder than people who did not suffer this way.

This led to what I called 'Psychological Tunnel Vision' (PTV). It was as if the person's perception was like a torch with a narrow beam and they only saw what was within the beam of light.

This PTV led to the sufferers seeing only the task in hand and even then the object of their concentration was often just a blur. The PTV in its turn became a problem and the sufferer found they were succeeding less and less in even the simplest of tasks and involved in more and more accidental occurrences.

Like the snowball rolling down the hill the whole problem became bigger and bigger And served to increase the lack of confidence the person had.

This to me was like the fight or flight syndrome and led me to coin the phrase 'Slow Panic'.

The more I studied these people and their problem the more I began to realise that their accident proneness was because they did not see outside the task in hand, it was almost as if the periphery of their visual field did not exist outside of anything they tried to concentrate on. Putting all this data together and wanting to help these people, I came up with an exercise I thought would help.

When I was confronted with a person who had a confidence problem I told them they had formed a bad habit of seeing incorrectly and had produced PTV in their day to day behaviour. I told them it took three to four weeks of concentrated effort to change a bad habit and cited exercises where people had changed harmless habits like putting a particular leg or arm in their apparel first when dressing . (Psycho Cybernetics, 1960Maxwell Maltz, MD.,FICS.)

I then reminded them that it took approximately three to four weeks to change a habit. I requested they do this simple exercise several times a day for four weeks. I even helped out when I felt it necessary to establish a programme to ensure they did not miss any opportunity to do the exercise.

Without exception all those people who did things correctly reported back that their lives had become easier, they were less accident prone and their solutions to problems seemed more efficient. (They had changed their habitual way of seeing.)

They also reported a greater feeling of wellbeing and easing of general tension that in some cases had become a physical feeling that they had learned to live with.

This obviously gave me a great sense of achievement and I assumed their feeling of wellbeing was a natural reaction to the easing of life's trials and tribulations.

I began to feel however that the difference the exercise seemed to make to the lives of some of those people appeared to be too great and that maybe they were over reacting.

This made me feel there was a danger they may face some sort of trauma some day and not only go back to square one but even become worse than they had been when I first met them.

Even more dangerous, this may reinforce their original problems and make them irreversible. Whilst I felt that I could not stop offering this kind of help to people I also felt the need to investigate further.

The reading I did from here on would require thinking about very carefully so I looked again at the personalities I had been asking to do the exercise I had devised.

Whilst attempting to live their lives as normal as possible these people all previously showed some if not all of the following behaviour.

I had already noted that these people had the habit of looking down at the ground rather than looking other people in the eye. On further examination I realised these people also hid themselves away when there was not a pressing need to interact with others.

They would stay in their room and not communicate if there was no need to do so. They would even keep the curtains closed which seemingly symbolically kept the world out and they would stay in bed and sleep as much as possible. If they were active in any way they tended to choose solitary pursuits that required little or no interaction with others.

In short their behaviour was typically withdrawal from the world as much as possible until they looked for help. ie. Depressive behaviour.

They chose varying degrees of these behaviours and did not seem to follow all of them. The more of these behaviours they displayed the more likely it was that they were Introduced to me by relatives or a friend, if they had managed to find one in their lives.

Being aware of the existence of Manic Depression and it's symptoms I was sensitive to the condition of the people who described what appeared to be the greatest amount of feeling of wellbeing after a period of doing the exercise.

I decided to look again into what the person would experience during the exercise in order to guide me in my further reading and study.

I realised that by making the person look up rather than down and then to concentrate on broadening their visual field I was making them let more light in to their system.

I visited a friend during this period and he had a Budgerigar in a cage. The bird was very noisy and he was finding it hard to concentrate on our conversation so he draped a cloth over the cage and the bird immediately went quiet.

This led me to start to study animals that hibernate. They either go south from the Northern hemisphere (presumably to seek more light) or capitulate and go to sleep for the winter. I discovered from this that Serotonin or the lack of it was involved in this process. I read that other behaviour was affected and that animals become more active at certain times.

What I read was that when a body is subjected to sunlight Serotonin is produced within that body and it becomes more active. With the light there is also heat and when the sun produces more heat creatures like my Goldfish in the pond require feeding more often.

Conversely when there is less light the body slows down and people who tend to be more sensitive to the lack of light begin to feel depressed.

Having looked thoroughly into this I started to ask people who were depressed to do my exercise. These people did respond positively and being concerned only with helping them I started treating depressives in this way.I was only interested in helping people, I was not looking for kudos or fame so I did not seek publicity of any sort. Some years later I read in a newspaper that the Americans had discovered something they called 'SAD' (Seasonal Affected Disorder) and were producing light boxes to treat people.

That is fine as long as the people who need it are getting some sort of affective and positive treatment they can afford then I am happy. Perhaps I was a little short sighted and should have sought publicity so that more people were able to benefit from what I had discovered. If this treatise is published then I would have achieved this and may end up helping many more.

In opening my 'Hypnotherapy Business' I insisted on having a separate office which was perceived as professional and not trying to cut costs by running it from my home as so many people tried to do. I had joined the institute which had run the Hypnotherapy course I had taken and I now concentrated on being successful.

I advertised and travelled around the area giving talks to local groups and after becoming well established and well known I was even invited to a local psychiatric Hospital to talk to the staff about my business and my methods.

I was also asked by my institute to give talks at institute meetings because some of my colleagues were sending their clients to me when they were people who had particularly difficult psychological problems.

Success however brings it's own particular problems and I had three problems, only one of which I recognised as a possibility. The other two were somewhat of a surprise in their way and caught me unawares.

The first of these problems was something that I was aware of as a possibility. I would sometimes get clients who complained about one of my fellow practitioners in other practices. They would complain mostly of sexual misconduct. I would ask only one question and that was how many times had they visited this practitioner. The number of visits would give me an idea, along with any other complainants if they existed, as to the truth of the matter.

Transference * is a known occurrence and the more visits the client had made to the practitioner the more likely that it could be transference.

I would then have an idea as to whether I should investigate further or not.

Having got my answer I would then disregard the complaint after assuring the client that it would be dealt with by the institute. I would then ask the client what their problem was that had taken them along to see a practitioner and proceed to help them any way I could to overcome that problem. This somewhat immediate action often meant that the other practitioner was forgotten along with the associated problem.

I was fully aware that transference could claim me as a victim at any time so I endeavoured to have my receptionist in the building and highly visible, whilst not entering my consulting room, at all times. I also encouraged my receptionist to tell the client that I was very good at my job but I always insisted that she mention that I had a lovely wife and children. This had a dual effect, it increased the possibility that my client would get benefit because it discouraged them from questioning me and the things I said. It also had the effect of putting up a barrier in the clients mind if they did start to get inappropriate feeling towards me.

Unfortunately when she was my receptionist my Wife often forgot to mention that she was my Wife or told the people that we had problems but that I was so good she could not say hurtful things about me. This she may have thought reinforced just how good I must be at my job. I knew this because some of my clients told me so with comments like, "That receptionist is either your wife, or wants to be, the things she says about you." or, "How can you have problems with your wife when she thinks so much of you."

This of course backfired because it encouraged clients to allow themselves to have feeling for me rather than to discourage them. Eventually one or two lonely ladies must have fallen in love with me and, unlike me, my fellow practitioners encouraged them to talk about it so they could do something about it armed with as much information as they could get.. This had the effect of increasing the inappropriate feelings and made the unfortunate ladies more unhappy because I showed no return of their feelings.

At the time this problem became a difficulty for me I did not even consider what my Wife had done. Later however I must admit I did wonder whether she had done this deliberately or not, because she was at that time having an affair with someone I had thought was a friend. This I consider was two problems rolled into one even bigger problem.

My other problem at that time was a little more complicated and came from within the Professional Institute.

I had become well known and even revered among my institute colleagues because of my talks and my reputation that compelled them to send people with very complicated problems to me to be helped.

The constitution of the Institute stipulated that the President had to put himself up for election every five years and that time was coming up. Some of my colleagues had rung me and asked me to stand against him, some in very definite and strong terms.

I had not mentioned this to the president but one day during a phone conversation, completely out of the blue, he mentioned the upcoming election and said I was the only person in the institute capable of doing the job and winning the election against him. I was somewhat surprised that he brought the subject up and when he asked me not to stand I said I would consider his request. I contacted one of the more vociferous people who wanted me to stand and told him what had happened. He then informed me that the current president was at that moment under investigation by the police for *misuse of the Institute funds*. Apparently he was resisting all their efforts and the police were struggling so would I approach the police and see what way I may be able to help them. When I was able to speak to the police man in charge he informed me that he was certain that the president was guilty but could not persuade the bank to release the accounts for them to study.

It was at this time that I heard rumours about my conduct with my clients. I immediately went to my own local police and asked them to investigate these rumours which were of a criminal nature. There were two officers put on to the case and the female officer was very anti and nasty to me the moment I met her.

In spite of her attitude, on completion of their apparently very thorough and rigorous work, they told me I was innocent of any wrong doing.

In the meantime the president of the institute, determined to hide his own misdemeanours and cause a smokescreen that would involve me and get me out of the running, had involved the newspapers. He held a

Kangeroo court and made sure the newspapers were present outside and were given the 'so called' verdict so they could print it in the next national edition.

The newspapers, struggling for a story that would sell more copies fell on me like a pack of wolves. They deliberately made me angry and then photographed me. They printed only my eyes narrowed in anger and included the headline which said 'The eyes of evil'. I could do nothing about it. They then printed whole pages of tabloid papers. The first sentence in every edition proclaimed my innocence which was true but the rest of the article was included to make the readers forget that sentence. They printed whole pages of the so called accusations against me. These fabrications were very heavy on words and served to blank out the memory of that first sentence. The readers accordingly only remembered the accusations as if they were the truth.

This proved to be my sentence of guilt even though the police had stated otherwise.

The Institute hearing included half a dozen people who had all been subject of sexual complaints, that I had dealt with, but had crawled back begging forgiveness from the president. I have no doubt they were under orders from the president and they ignored my statements. The president then expelled me from the institute.

I had many clients who had done my exercises and taken my advice and gained help from their efforts. They had cured themselves by doing these things but now if they heard and believed these lies about me they were in danger of losing all that they had gained. Not only this but I could not even consider continuing my work. I had already had women approach me for sexual favours in my practice because of what they had come to believe and I was forced to discontinue and go back into engineering for my lively hood.

In this way I hoped I would save at least some of my previous clients from sliding back into their problems when I disappeared from public view.

This change in my lifestyle led to my meeting my third and best (by a million miles) Wife who makes me very happy indeed. Unfortunately I have been unable to carry on the work which may have helped many, many other people. I sincerely hope that this work gets published and may help to produce a change, hopefully, so the world in general starts to get some benefit by learning my exercise and making themselves able to get the best out of their lives.

- *'Transference '– If a client begins to feel they are over, or have overcome, their problem because of a practitioner, their feelings of being grateful sometime become what they feel is love for that practitioner. This will then create new problems within their lives.*

# Sarah and Brenda

*This chapter could be called 'Chalk and Cheese.' Sarah being excellent as Chalk and cheese being the other end of the good/bad spectrum.*

I had a practice in psychotherapy using hypnosis as one of my main tools and I was very successful.

Evil people railed against me and my therapy practice. I call them evil because the main protagonists were more self- concerned than anything else. The others were just weak unfortunate people who knew not what they were doing and were also only concerned with being scorned lovers. (Not that they were ever actual lovers, only wannabees.)

The president of our Professional Institute was up for re-election and was being investigated by the Police for 'misuse of institute funds'. Both he and a number of others told me that my high profile within the institute and the apparent esteem with which I was held made me the only person who could be considered to replace the current President.

The Police Officer in charge of the investigation informed me that the President was definitely guilty of the misdemeanour but the accounts of the institute were required in order to reveal the necessary evidence. Unfortunately, somehow the president was able to prevent the bank from producing them and the Police could not go forward with the case.

Of course this withholding of the evidence was one of the indicators of guilt on the part of the Institute President. I often wonder how it is that the bank was not found complicit by sticking to some rule or other and therefor protecting a criminal by aiding and abetting him in avoiding justice in his crime.

Had I been voted in as the next president the police would have received a copy of the accounts and the prosecution could have gone ahead.

This situation prompted the incumbent president to falsify a case against me to discredit me and therefor put me in a position where I could not be voted in as President.

Various stories had been cobbled together about my alleged misuse of my practice to take advantage of my clients. As I remember I was not awarded the Kudos of picking attractive people to insult.

I went to the police and requested them to investigate the allegations against me in order for them to prove my innocents of any wrong doing. The Police did this but then refused to make a public statement accordingly.

The president got together a bunch of miscreants who had all been either removed from the Institute or heavily censured for their own misdemeanours and were all desperate to get back into his good books.

*I had dealt with complaints about most of these people and when a client made a complaint against one of my colleagues I would gather information from the client and pass it on to the Institute. I would then enquire what the clients problem was, assure them their complaint was being dealt with and immediately start to discuss the problem they had sought treatment for and concentrate on that. This way the client felt everything including their complaint was being dealt with, let the professionals deal with that aspect, and settled into dealing with their original problem bringing equilibrium and peace to their lives.*

The President then convened a Kangaroo court situation with these miscreant characters as a so called panel (Jury) and demanded my presence in a very public place.

There was no real case as the police had found from their investigation but they found me to have acted incorrectly and the president was able to pronounce my dismissal from the institute and get me out of his hair. The other aspect of this was of course he was able to get these miscreant back on side and being favourable to him because he had re-legitimised them and allowed them to start earning once again at a more favourable monetary level.

He could also claim to have increased by a little the membership of the institute giving him some kudos with members who were not aware of the political shenanigans of the more senior people around them.

He also made sure that he had national newspaper reporters there who then chased me for my comments and followed up by publishing what they safely could, which served to make me look like a guilty man and sold many newspapers around the country.

Their tactic was to start their articles with a short sentence stating my innocence then to follow up with a long and wordy statement of my alleged crimes. By the time people had read to the end of the article they had effectively forgotten the first line and only remembered the most comprehensive list of lying allegations that followed.

This whole process was carried out with no regard to the many people who had taken my advice and cured themselves of many ill's. This meant that if these people became aware of what was said and began to doubt my honour, uprightness and good character then their cures would just disappear like smoke in the wind. I was left with no alternative but to disappear from the public eye in the hopes that as few people as possible would learn of this charade and hopefully retain their equilibrium and their cures for the rest of their lives. I was desperate that they would not regain the pain they had lived with before they met me. Having an alternative career as an Engineer I went back to it and quietly disappeared from the public view.

During the whole of the previously described process there was another scenario playing out in my life which it seems, being known by many people of my acquaintance, was lending an air of apparent reality and background to the allegations which must have made some people think that some, at least, of the allegations against me were true because of the conditions I was living under. My Wife was having an affair and deliberately trying to ensure my marriage would break down.

Knowing this and trying to prepare for the consequences I had met a young lady who had more goodness in her little finger than all the people involved in the above mentioned charade put together.

Initially the only place we could meet in any privacy was in my office and one of the people who fed misinformation to the Institute President was a lady who was about forty years my senior and had suffered what is called * 'transference' and was secretly in love with me.

This lady was working with me as a volunteer receptionist and knew of my situation and approached the institute in some vain hope of turning things to her benefit. This of course fell right into the eager hands of the Institute President at the most opportune time for him, but not for me. However I had met Sarah and was preparing for a life with her.

When the lies and rumours about me started to emerge, another lady, (I shall call Brenda) heard of me and made an appointment to see me.

When she entered my office I was struck by her seeming high emotional state and prepared myself to listen to her story.

Unfortunately all she wanted was to persuade me to have sex with her because of the rumours she'd heard. I informed her, as gently and kindly as I could, that was not part of my job description.

I made no charge and showed her the door. I do not know what she said to the old lady who was acting as my volunteer receptionist at the time but she was still there in the reception when my next client arrived some time later and seemed totally unembarrassed or worried at seeing me when I went into the reception to collect the next client.

At about that time my Wife admitted adultery so that I could divorce her and start the process of settling down with my new partner. In this process I discovered that my new partners mother was unfortunately a year younger than I.

In spite of my having my own house and good earning potential and being a hard working person, my partners Mother disinherited her and started to withdraw from her life. This meant that in spite of a mutual enjoyment of golf between my partners Mother and Father and myself, I *(the gold digger)* was never invited to join them on the golf course. My partners Sisters boyfriend however hated golf and did not wish to play but was almost manhandled into the golf club and ended up having lessons.

My partner was invited to her family home once or twice but then the invitations dried up. On one of these occasions I happened to be present because I was in the house when my partners Mother came home, with her Mother, from a shopping spree and my partner was there to see her Grandmother. My partners Father was working away as an advisor to the military and was in a dangerous area of the world at that time.

My partners Mother revealed her attitude to her husband's situation by a startling statement. Her Daughters questioned her about the relatively large amount of money she had spent on shopping, some items of which were somewhat frivolous. I commented that maybe it took her mind off the fact that her Husband was working in an area abroad in which there was a large amount of terrorist activities. The Grandmother agreed somewhat but still questioned the amount of money spent and asked her daughter to defend herself.

My partners Mother then made a comment which glued itself into my mind forever. She said, "I don't care where my husband is or what is happening to him as long as he keeps sending me lots of lovely money to spend in any way I wish."

My children lived some distance away and without my partners family who lived close, but were not interested, we were left to make our own entertainment even at Christmas and birthdays when she did not even get greeting cards. This whole scenario with my partners family hurt me a great deal and had me worried about her future. Being that much older than her and not being able to guarantee our future relationship which may include my early demise leaving her alone and lonely I worried greatly about our relationship.

In the end I decided that I could cause her, and myself, one quick great pain and give her time to get back into the bosom of her family or I could selfishly hang on to her and maybe guarantee her a long, lonely and painful old age. I hated the idea because of my feelings for her and what it may do to both of us for a while, but I decided it would be in her best interest if we broke up our relationship. I broke the news to Sarah about my decision and there followed a session where we both cried like babies, her begging me not to do it and me pleading that I could not put her in the position that we both wanted so much. If I had known that we could be together for at least twenty five and maybe even thirty years or more I would not have acted as I did but I would have been selfish to even try.

I contacted Brenda from my records and arranged a meeting. She was a very attractive woman and the inevitable happened. We began a relationship and I made sure Sarah was informed of what had occurred to try and give her some justification for what was happening. I felt cruel and I felt like a criminal for what I did but even now I feel that I released her and I would desperately like to hear that she is back with the worthwhile members of her family and finding some happiness with someone in her life.

Meanwhile I kept up my relationship with Brenda and allowed her to use and abuse me in her very selfish way. Psychology had been my hobby before I even knew the word existed. It had started in the bomb shelters of the east end of London during World War Two and still persists today. Brenda already had a degree from some university or other and stated that she wanted to get another but this time in psychology. She enrolled, I lent her a word processor and started to tutor her unofficially by discussing her assignments with her and helping her to shape any work she did including her final thesis. She ended up with a two one degree and said, very smugly well I always knew I could. What she did with her degree I know not, nor do I care.

I only know that whilst I was with her I did a great deal of work in her house as well and in the finish I was discarded like an old rag that she seemed to despise.

I installed a hand rail in a staircase leading to her loft, I constructed a built in wardrobe in a bedroom, I erected approximately sixty feet of trellis around her back garden, I built a mobile plinth to increase the height of a double bed that was too low and I did many small jobs around the house.

When all this was finished and she had her new degree she ended the affair and refused to hand back my word processor which she claimed I had given to her as a present. This in spite of a local policeman she had called, because I was being a nuisance, telling her she should return the word processor to me forthwith.

I ended up abandoning the word processor, which was old anyway, and vowing to never say a good word for the lady (?) ever again. Even so I changed her name for use in this true story of my life which needed telling.

# A Hard Winter

In 1959 being unaware that I had been tricked into a marriage I carried on working in construction in order to get a good qualification. This meant that I faced the possibility of having no work in construction over the next winter so I would have to look elsewhere for gainful employment. (In those days there were no additives for cement to prevent it from freezing during cold weather so many construction sites would close down for the season.)

Fortunately I was given the chance to work with a company who dealt in precious metals. This work was extremely hard but paid fantastically well if you could keep at it. I got the job and when I started work I was informed by the foreman that I would be grade four for seniority and payment. If I did well and was fortunate I could be lifted to grade three in six months, and it would take a year for me to reach grade two if I was lucky. He started this statement with, "You are a bit small but you seem intelligent so……"

The company ran a three shift system and if the company were informed that a person on the next shift after yours would not be arriving it was not unusual for them to ask you to work a second shift as a replacement.

At the end of the first week the Foreman asked me to work with him on a job involving long handled steel ladles. These ladles although being of heavy grade steel would have holes in them that appeared after a short period of use on molten metal. To replace the whole ladle would be very expensive so the idea was to cut of the head, or bowl, and replace only that.

What happened was the ladle had been heated to a red colour in a furnace. The foreman held the ladle by the handle and placed it on a chisel which was placed in a square hole in an anvil. The chisel being against the bowl as close as possible and I had to hit the handle on top of the chisel

113

so the handle was cut through and the bowl fell off. The foreman told me I should try to equal what he called 'Big George's record'. This was to cut off the bowl in one hit, obviously you could not do better but no one else had been able to equal it.

George was a big Jamaican man who had muscles on his arms as big as my head. My technique was to aim just past the target and at the last second to pull the hammer in to the target. This had the effect of increasing the power of the blow and two hits made the job easier than normal. I used more power and one hit was indeed sufficient to do the job.

There were fourteen or fifteen ladles and, becoming enthusiastic, I finished them all in one blow each but on the penultimate ladle my enthusiasm got the better of me and I pulled the hammer too much. This meant the hammer slid off the chisel on my side and it hit the edge of the anvil. As this happened I felt a blow on my shin. I obviously had not hit myself with the hammer but I staggered and when we examined my leg there was a small thin red line and some pain.

We concluded there was very little damage so I finished the job. Unfortunately I could not walk very easily so the foreman insisted I go and visit the first aid station to ensure the incident got reported and he verified the circumstances.

The first aid man looked at the spot with a magnifying glass and declared there was nothing in the wound so it was very minor, stuck a plaster on it and sent me on my way. The pain however got worse and the next morning I went to my Doctor who sent me off to the Hospital for an ex-ray. The ex-ray showed a piece of what turned out to be the edge of the anvil which had entered my leg so fast it had hit one bone and deflected behind the other.

We had not even considered that an anvil could be broken in this way so of course we had not thought of such a thing. I was thinking, wrongly, that maybe part of an old weld where the old bowl had been fixed had broken off.

The Doctors decided that because of my pain the piece may be moving and this endangered all the blood vessels and tendons that ran down the back of my leg. This could make me permanently disabled so the piece had to be removed. Unfortunately because of the tendons etc. in the back of my leg the surgeon would have to go into my leg from the front.

This meant that the scar would be very large for such a small object.

I was lying on a trolley and having strapped my leg to the trolley they injected me with a local anaesthetic. After allowing a certain amount of time the Doctor started to cut into my leg. I informed him that I could feel pain from what he was doing and he ignored me. I tried to tell him again and sat up whilst doing it. This was when I realised he was cutting me what I considered was the wrong way, because I had seen the ex-ray photograph.

His reply was that he was the doctor and could interpret the ex-ray better than I. I informed him that when he gave up his attempt at retrieving the metal because it was not possible I, being angry with his incompetents, would make him pay for it.

He had progressively added more nurses to my body starting with one on my other leg then, one on my head, then one on my chest, then one on each of my arms in order to hold me down and, I suspect, ensure I could not get to him when he final gave in and admitted he had failed.

When he did finally admit they had to now send me to a ward and apply a general anaesthetic and cut the other way I lost my temper and the nurses all went in different directions as I reared up and struck him on the chin.

After the operation and they had produced a 'T' shaped scar, cutting a muscle into three pieces, they informed me the muscle may never heal properly so I may never be able to play football again.

I did eventually play football again but this was not the end of this sorry tale.I often call myself 'The nearly man', because I somehow miss out by a hairs breadth when aiming for things. The corollary to this is that it always seemed to be the fault of something else as opposed to my doing.

The company paid me full pay whilst I was off sick, acknowledging that the equipment was faulty and not me. I therefor went to the local employment office and asked them to approach the company for some compensation, partly because I had been told that I would never be fit enough again to play sport.

They said it was not their responsibility as this was a closed shop union company. They advised me to approach the union who would apply on my behalf.

Before the accident I had been told that I had to join the union or I would lose the job because they would not allow a non- union worker to work alongside their union colleagues.

I asked who the union representative was and I was told, the rep for my shift was on holiday so I had to wait for him to return. The reference to 'my shift' led me to think I could speak to the Union rep. on the next shift so I stayed behind after my shift and approached him.

He refused to do anything for me and referred me back to my own shift rep..

Having had the accident, and before being declared fit to return to work, I sought out the union rep and filled out the application for membership, as required.

When I approached the union they refused to do anything for me. I asked why and they said I had not been a member of the union when the accident occurred. I informed them of the circumstances and referred them to their union representatives involved but they still refused to give me any help.

I went back to the local employment office and they told me it was nothing to do with them and refused to even talk to me about my case. Not knowing what to do next and having a pregnant Wife I could not fight the company for fear of losing the job, so I stayed on. After two months and well before the first year was up I was made up to grade two on the strength of my hard work and intelligent approach to the work, I was told.

When the winter was over, and construction work became available again, I left the company to go back to the work I preferred. When I gave my notice to the Manager, he tried to persuade me to stay. I told him what he could do with his job and his company and he seemed not to understand why.

# On The Buses

The nearest main bus route to where I lived, after moving out of the London dock area, was the Hertford road. Going, in to, London the road obviously started at Hertford. For the longest distance on the road, two of the buses that ran were the 249 and the 649.

This chapter is not in chronological order, it starts at the longest distance from London and works its way towards the centre. It does not cover the whole distance, only the places where things happened to me that I felt were interesting, but not in chronological order.

Starting in Cheshunt I went there on a few occasions to fish as a child and on one occasion to visit my first Wife's Sister, nothing to report.

Waltham Cross and Waltham Abbey, often visited, sometime to fish in the nearby River Lea and in my teenage years I went often to two public houses, The Castle and The Oak. These pubs were run by a Friend's Father. The friend Garry Pringle was introduced to me by my, best friend's Brother Jack. I believe it was in this area that Jack met Fran. She was a Cousin of Hellen Shapiro, the pop singer. I believe this came about because of another singer who was about to gain a certain amount of fame. He was sometimes in evidence and his name was Harry Web, (A.K.A. Cliff Richard.) Harry and I were both born in the same year, Nineteen-Forty.

A year or two later, a group of young people, who were Elvis fans, were extolling the virtues of Elvis. The leader of the group said, "Anyone who is not a fan of Elvis, is going to be beaten up." He then asked one or two people if they were Elvis fans and they all said, I thought in fear, that they loved Elvis, maybe they did, but that had become irrelevant, in the circumstances.

117

When the leader turned to me and asked the same question, refusing to allow myself to be bullied, I told the truth of my feelings and said," I am a fan of Elvis of course, but I Would not be surprised if Cliff outlives Elvis's fame and is around a lot longer." The bully seemed non-plussed but did not argue, he seemed lost for words.

In the interim between the times in the Waltham's and the Elvis fans incidence, I had two other memorable happenings with Gary. On one trip from Enfield, via Chingford, we were travelling, in Gary's car along a road called, Sewardstone Road, and the back door on one side of the car had a broken lock. The road was somewhat of a Country road and very winding. I was requested to hold the door close but the forces were very strong and I ended up stretching across, holding the handles on both doors either side of the car and having my shoulders feeling as if someone was trying to wrench then out of their sockets, but Gary was not about to slow down because he was late.

At another time we were again in Gary's car, with the doors repaired, we were proceeding past Ryance Park, which was on the Ponders End stretch of the Hertford Road, which was also called Ponders End High Street.

We were heading towards London and had just passed the police station, it had started to snow and there was about two inches (five millimetres) of thickness, on the road. There is also a slow bend at that point, and Gary, somewhat unwisely, tried to speed up. The net result was that we did a complete waltz turn in the road and ended up still going in the same direction with no further incident. We both laughed and Gary started trying to make it happen again, but the road was now straight, and it would not happen again.

Continuing along the Hertford road out of Waltham Cross, and in to Enfield Highway, there is Albany Park on the left, and opposite the park was a public house called the White Horse, and next to the park before it was a cinema called The Rialto. The pub was quite large and had a hut next to it which was used for various functions. The hut was timber on the outside and painted plaster board on the inside. It was perfect for a club to hire as their venue to hold its meeting's.

A couple called Judy and Eric, hired it to turn it into a Judo Club. Eric was a Black belt and Judy was a Blue belt. The couple used the club for their own practice and to try to increase Judy's belt colour. During club evenings the members were given a short break to help them recover from, sometime strenuous, workouts. When this occurred Eric and Judy would carry out some throws to let their students see how it was done. During these sessions it became known that Judy would often grab Eric's long, black hair and use it to throw him. This was done to show females that if ever they needed to practice, self- defence, they could use their, opponents hair to their benefit in order to save themselves in any given situation.

I joined the club and learned a lot, including some throws above my grade, which could be useful in the future, if required. Unfortunately, one night Judy got too enthusiastic and grabbing Eric's hair, she threw him straight through the clubhouse wall. The owners of the building said their insurance did not cover for, what they called, 'That type of deliberate violence.' So, Eric and Judy had to pay for the damage or get out. The result of that was that the club disappeared and I had to find some other activity to amuse me.

# A Trip Up Country

I was fifteen years old. I had run away from home. I was not a bad child, I was running from the expectation that I would have to attend the hospital every day in order to watch and listen as my Mother slowly, and painfully, died of Lung Cancer. She lay in a bed and her skin had darkened. She was unconscious and the only sound she made was her very laboured breathing and the occasional moan from the pain which seemed to invade her conscious body through the unconscious reality of her being. Her body looked like bare bones covered with nothing but her unhealthy, darkened, skin. If a photograph had been taken of this poor, suffering person, a viewer would be forgiven for thinking it was a horrendous tableau dreamed up and executed by a sick mind.

What was the cause of this terrible dilemma that I and my family were enduring?

Was it industrialisation that was the main cause of London's pollution, particularly in the, ever busy, dockland area? Part of that pollution was of course the fuel used by ordinary people to cook and warm their homes and transport themselves, from place to place, in their daily lives. Was it the smog, which was just normal fog, which held the pollution, at ground level where it could have such a devastating effect upon people? Was it the two world wars during which so many buildings were turned to, dust? After all, most if, not all, of those buildings had asbestos built in by well meaning constructors who did not realise its harmful effect on the lungs of people. Of course, the straw which broke the camel's back was the excessive smoking that my poor Mother indulged in. Let's face it, even the medical profession, in those days, did not fully understand the harm cigarette smoking could do to the bodies of those who indulged. Also, if you lived in a dock area and had the right sort of friends, you would find it easy to obtain the hard to come by items, like cigarettes during a war time period, and my mother had many good friends.

She ended up smoking something like sixty cigarettes a day. I well remember, when their usual brand of cigarettes were scarce, my Mother would come home with foreign brands which smelt very different, so much so that my father could not stand them and he would say to my Mother, "Oh no, you have not got those things again." She would just giggle and light one up so that he complained even more.

When she started to complain about the pain in her left breast, in about my seventh or eighth year, it was not associated with her lungs, she thought and said it was in her breast.

When I was nine I had a bout of, what my Doctor called quinze's, and my Mother took me to see him because I did not feel well enough to go to school. When the Doctor had pronounced about my condition my, Mother, asked him about her pain, for the first time. I was still in the room and the Doctor started to treat my Mother but, he remembered I was there and asked me to go and wait in the waiting room whilst he examined my Mother.

The result of this was that my Mother visited the local hospital and after ex-raying her they pronounced that she had a shadow on her lung and started the long bout of treatment that she went through.

As a family, all we could do during those visits in her final year of life, was to sit in silence, with maybe an occasional comment, and watch, listen and suffer, sharing her pain.

For me this was so painful and difficult that I hit on the solution of running away. If I was not present at hospital visiting times, I could not be expected to go and indulge in this torture.

---

When I left home on these occasions, I would often make my way to the west end of London, where I could easily mingle without being found and taken back. One of my regular haunts at this time, was a particular night club, in Soho.

On a particular night at this club, I witnessed what I was certain was the murder of a man who had been targeted by a drug addicted prostitute and her friends, who were similarly, under the influence of drugs.

I managed to leave the scene without becoming involved and determined that I would keep away for some time until any resulting investigations were complete. I went to other clubs for a short period, but unfortunately, as was not uncommon at that time, I became involved in another incident. This time I was the target of someone in a happening which I had been told occurred regularly, but normally with females. Historically the following short note, explains its relevance to the next story.

A previous happening in which I was involved, at the same Soho club, was on a night when it was very crowded. I shared a table with another male whose face was familiar, from previous visits. This night however, even though he like me was not of legal age to indulge in alcohol, he was drinking and becoming intoxicated. He kept brushing tears from his eyes, and I began to feel sorry for him. After a while I asked him if he was alright, and he proceeded to tell me his tale of woe.

Apparently, his boyfriend had become angry, for no apparent reason, and had kicked him out of their flat, telling him not to return. Although we did not become close friends, we did become friendly and always passed the time of day with each other, whenever we met.

One night, the club was quite dead, and we were bored. We were sitting at different tables, and he came over and said he was going to a different club, in Bayswater, and would I like to go with him. I explained that I was short of funds and did not want to spend money on transport. He told me, he had made up with his boyfriend and he was going to arrive shortly to take him to Bayswater in his car, so I was welcome to join him.

I knew the barman at the Bayswater club, who had attended the same school as myself, and would later marry the club owner, although I did not know this at that time. We were obviously not of the same age but he was well known, at the school and I was also well known because of my name and he was a friend of my older brother. I agreed to accept the lift, and when the, 'Boyfriend,' turned up, I was surprised to find he was a, well known, figure who some referred to as, 'The King of London's Underworld.' When we arrived at the club we split up and I had a good evening.

The incident which makes the above story relevant is as follows.

One of the clubs I was visiting as a change, to keep me out of sight for a short time, was situated at the end of a narrow alley, which became very dark after nightfall. Some way into this alley was a short bit that was wider, and I was approaching the club in the dark.

Suddenly I was grabbed and dragged aside. A voice said, "Right, I'm arresting you for soliciting." I was totally shocked and laughed, thinking it must be a friend who was having a joke with me.

The voice said, "This is no joke, boy. Do as you are told or face the consequences." I said, "You've made a mistake mate." he said, "Do you Want to go inside." I said, "What the hell are you talking about, you must be daft. I bet your not even a copper." he said, "Oh I'm a copper alright and I've seen you being friendly with the boyfriend of our underworld king, so, if you don't let me '$*?%' you (Have sex with you) I'll have you down the station and booked in, in no time, sunshine." I said, You've got no chance, I'm not a poof and no one, gets near making me one, whoever you are, take me down the station if you want." He then said, "If I do, and you go inside, you will become a poof in no time, so you might as well let me do it now to save time." As he said, this I heard, what sounded like a couple talking and giggling together, enter the alley.

He was still holding my wrist, but I was able to pull back and I aimed a kick at what I thought was about his crutch area. I must have been quite close because he groaned loudly and let me go. I immediately turned and ran towards the road. I connected with what seemed like a man's arm but kept on running. I turned onto the main road as I left the alley and kept running, I took the next corner and then another corner and then a third corner. I saw a bus stop a short distance away and ran to it. I kept looking behind me until a bus came and being sure he was not following me I climbed on board and rode for two stops. Then sought out the nearest underground station and, using the tube, made my way to Stamford hill, on the Hartford Road.

From there I made my way to South Tottenham Station and spent a week in the area, sleeping in the station waiting room, on the same road each night.

Still feeling very vulnerable, I managed to get a job, helping out in a wet fish shop and sleeping in the flat above, until I had accumulated a small amount of cash. I still felt unsafe so, I resigned and started my journey up country to get away from London. Shortly after this, the police found me and took me back to London. They interviewed me with my Father present and he said he thought my grandfather, who was a ships Captain I had never met, had caused my Wanderlust. The police concluded that I could not be 'cured', so asked my Father if he thought I would benefit by a custodial sentence, what they actually said was, "We have a house where he will be comfortable and will learn how to live right among other people." He agreed, so I was taken into custody and spent a year in an Approved School. I met some evil people in there, but managed to remain a good person so that on leaving, I was strong enough to face the trials and tribulations the world subsequently threw at me, and they have been many.

On other occasions, when leaving home, I would head up north. In so doing I visited many new places, each producing its own story, most of which were not worthy of mention.

There were of course one or two stories of note. One time I had got myself a lift, in a lorry, across the Pennines, in deep snow, in the winter. As we went slowly along the road I saw sheep looking over the dry-stone wall at us, and others clustering against mine ventilation shafts which allowed the ingress of oxygenated air to the mine and a certain amount of pollution release from the mines. This pollution release was obviously a little warmer, hence the groups of sheep close to them.

On two occasions however, the sheep looking over the wall at us seemed to just disappear, in an instant. On the second occasion of this happening, I mentioned it to the driver and he informed me that, it was so cold they just died and dropped on the spot.

On another occasion, I had obtained a job as a van drivers' mate. We made a delivery in Manchester and the next delivery was too far away to reach that day so we parked the van and the driver said we must walk to where we were going to stay for the night.

The walk took us through the centre of the town and through a famous arcade. When we were in the arcade it was very gloomy, and I was accosted by a young woman who offered me a good time for little cash. I had no cash and would not have availed myself of her services, mainly for the sake of my health. As we approached our destination, we went past a school which had an almost empty playground.

Two of the occupants, who I judged to be about twelve or thirteen, were leaning against the railings which surrounded the playground, and I could see quite clearly, the bare backside of the young girl, with her knickers pulled aside. They were having sex with no regard for what anyone passing could see.

On yet another occasion, up north, I was having a cup of tea in a, less than salubrious café. I overheard a person at the next table tell his companion that there was work to be had at a certain address in Edinburgh,

His companion poo pooed the idea on the grounds, it was too far away and by the time they got there, the job would be taken anyway.

I turned to them, apologised for listening in but said I was interested and where exactly was it? I was given the company name and told the road that it was in, but the person said it was a hundred miles away and not worth the bother.

Having no money and it being early morning, I decided to go for it.

I walked all day and all night and into the second day to get there. I knew I passed through Alnwick and Berrick on the way and the only sustenance I had was in the middle of the night when it was pitch black. I suddenly walked in to something on which I banged my knee, but not very hard. My knee was banged a second time because whatever I had hit came back and hit me again. I realised it was a water fountain, which were not uncommon in those days, in the middle of the town or village I was in at the time.

I immediately felt around in the dark until I found the button which released the water. I washed out the cup on the chain and filled it with water for one of the best drinks I ever had, cool and refreshing and beautiful.

I reached Edinburgh the next day, found the company by asking people and presenting myself to them, and set about asking for the job.

The man I spoke to said, "Sorry my friend I have just given it to the last applicant who starts in the morning."

Needless to say, I was somewhat devastated and looked for a park where I could sleep on a bench pretending to be a tourist.

# Friends And Acquaintances

Having been on this earth for over seventy years and being fairly well travelled I have met many people who have sometimes been friends and sometimes only acquaintances just like anyone else. Just like anybody else some of these people have been interesting as can be seen in the stories about 'Spitter Brown' and 'Mott Kettle'.

One of these people was a lady named Gladys Hoad, who later became Gladys Mc Burnie. Gladys and I met through my second wife, although I was already acquainted with her Brothers and their friends and associates. Gladys and I became close friends and I have loved her as such ever since we first met, although we do not see as much of each other now as we used to, I still feel the same about her.

A year or two after I met her Gladys went off to work in America for a time. Whilst there she sent home letters and in one letter she said she had become quite excited by a book she was reading and her excitement was because she said that every time she picked it up and started to read she kept getting a picture of me in her mind because it seemed to her that I was the subject of the book. She recommended I get a copy and read it myself but I could not find it in any bookshop at the time. However, she kept the book and brought it home with her and lent it to me to read. Sure enough, as I read it I felt as if a little man had entered my brain, taken notes, came out, wrote it all down and produced the book. It was quite eerie to wonder how much this man seemed to know about me.

Whilst I was reading the book Gladys rang me one day and told me that the author was in England and giving a talk about his book at the Savoy Hotel. She suggested we try to go to the talk and would I arrange tickets. The man who answered the phone to me was called George Hall and when taking my booking asked the reason I was interested and when I told him the story he requested I introduce myself to the Author and himself after the talk.

The Author was Doctor Maxwell Maltz, a well- known Plastic Surgeon. He claimed to have been involved in inventing the 'nose job'. It seemed he was intrigued because many of his patients having had physical scars removed used to go to him after the event and complain that the scar that had been removed was still there. In fact the scar had blighted their life and produced a mental scar which remained after the physical scar was gone. Max started an, in depth study of his patients and their condition and eventually realised that there self- image had become damaged and they did not know how to repair it so he set about finding a way they could do that. The result was his book, 'Psycho-Cybernetics' which was not only a way for people who had had plastic surgery to recover their true self- image but also an ideal method of self- improvement for anyone by boosting their self- image.

I was invited to meet Max in his suite at the Savoy after he had had a short break. When I arrived Max questioned me quite closely about his book and myself and he came to the conclusion that I would make a good Workshop Director in a self- improvement context. I attended some talks with other potential Workshop Directors and once the organisation were convinced we were ready we embarked upon a tour of lectures around London.

The format was, one person would give the talk and the others would form a panel to answer questions from the audience after this. We would take it in turns to give the talks so we all experienced this and the audience reaction later, which helped to give us confidence and to feel comfortable interacting with people in a lecture style situation. From these lectures we would recruit people into the lecture /interactive workshops.

The Workshop Directors were all qualified people other than myself. (luckily I had studied people and their psychology all my life from the second world war bomb shelters up until that time) My studies had been useful to me in forming my own personality and were the reason I had such a good rapport with the principals in the book.

I was in my late twenties and had a Mensa type IQ with a large practical element which I was able to bring to bear on the subject we were dealing with. One of my colleagues in this venture was Stewart Kipling who was a descendant of the great Rudyard Kipling and was also the

Managing Director of Aspro Nicholas the large drug company. Stewart was a Quaker and was very concerned with the well- being of others. He was a lovely man who I respected greatly.

At the time we were giving our talks around London the 'Scientology' movement were coming to the fore. Partly because of our name and partly because the subject matter was the mind and brain, people used to get confused so we were continually being asked if we were part of the Scientology movement. Whilst we were able to assure them we were not part of this movement we often discussed this anomaly at our regular Directors meetings.

We had agreed, with Max's okay, that in spite of the book title of 'Psycocybernetics' we would change the workshop title to, 'Human –Cybernetics' which seemed to suit the British market much better. We were hopeful that we would get rid of the confusion and in so doing would get a better response to our talks and consequent clientele.

As an aside, we also had problems at the talks with a man who kept turning up and causing problems from the audience. He had a companion who was in her twenties and very beautiful and did her best to hold him back when he played up. We were told this man was in fact, a plastic surgeon who had invented Liposuction. He was so good that his companion, 'in her twenties,' was in fact in her forties and was a sample of his genius. We were told that he disliked Max because Max had come to England many years before to teach him the nose job. Unfortunately however by the time he had learned enough to work on his own Max had taken the cream of the market, like the Marks sisters from Marks and Spencer's. So there was little for him to do to earn the big money because there were not too many people left who could afford to have the work done.

However George Hall was to prove to be our weakness. He would tell everyone that he had been a Principal Dancer for 'The Ballet Rambert' company in his young days and often spoke of the elderly ladies he was so fond of. These he had met at that time and was still acquainted with.

Because of the confusion and false links with scientology, which some people thought of at that time as a criminal organisation because of the claims that were made for it, there were investigations carried out by the authorities. I believe that an eminent Judge at that time ruled that Scientology was in fact a criminal organisation. These investigations, it seems, led to some sort of accusation against George and these were sufficient for people to back away and deny any connection with George whatever.

I never knew what the so called accusations against George were I was only told it was something to do with his old ladies. I was not able to contact any of the other people involved with our organisation at that time. I was only told George was the one person being considered and because of his association with psycho-Cybernetics his high profile within it had tainted it and everybody was too afraid to continue anymore and so it seemed to disappear without trace.

I never forgot the principals involved and, with some adjustment and reshaping I was able to use them to great benefit for others later in my practice in hypnotherapy and psychotherapy. This however came to grief for different reasons that were outside my control in spite of my innocence in the matter.

I have brushed up against quite a few high profile people in my time, mainly because my home base was London and I am certainly not alone or notable in this. I mention here one or two significant people but they may never even have registered my presence let alone remember me.

On one occasion I was driving out of a side street on to Oxford Street and as I approached the main road I was driving cautiously and was able to stop my car about an inch from a lady who it seems was more intent on her destination than she was on her final destiny and did not even consider the side road and any traffic that may appear from there.

The lady was called Millicent Martin and was at a very famous and high profile period in her life at that time. I do not think she even knew how close she came to serious injury at that juncture.

A similar incident occurred one day when I was carrying a very heavy engineer's tool bag. Again on Oxford street, and as I proceeded along the street towards my destination a man came out of a building and knocked into me.

The weight of the tool bag should have acted like ballast and held me in position but I was sent sideways and nearly lost my balance. This man was not much taller than me but he was as solid as a rock. I was young and quite fit in order to be able to carry such a heavy bag in the first place and this man had retired from the activity that had made him so famous and was consequently a lot older than me. He was Sterling Moss the world famous racing driver. Maybe he did not notice me but I cannot believe that, however he did not say a word and just kept on going so I doubt if he would even remember the incident.

Again with the same tool bag I was on the underground railway and one passenger who may have been late for work or an appointment was extremely rude to myself and others by, seemingly not even considering that other people existed. By luck, or otherwise, I ended up standing behind him on the escalator. Some how, my bag was protruding out in front of me and this man was trying to walk up, pushing people aside. It appears my bag was protruding so far that as he tried to lift his foot to push past the person in front of him, my bag caught his heel and he stumbled over. He spent the rest of his upwards journey trying to regain his feet and only succeeded when he reached the top.

I did not apologies but just walked away as if nothing had happened. I heard no commotion behind me and assume others thought he had got what he deserved and ignored him accordingly.

Yet again, with the same tool bag and travelling on an underground train, I was in a very crowded carriage and there was a heavily pregnant woman in front of me with her back to the door. The crowd were pushing against my back and I was worried I may not be able to keep from pushing up against her and injuring her or her baby. There was no room to put my bag down and this would have increased my weight if I fell onto her. The only thing I could think to do was to extend my free arm past her and lean on the door, keeping my arm straight.

Suddenly the woman started shouting at me and calling me names, saying I had touched her intimately, taking advantage of the situation. I protested and showed my other hand holding the tool bag whilst the hand all could see anyway was on the door behind her. It was obvious that it was not me, if anybody, who was the culprit. In spite of this I kept getting dirty looks from the other passengers for the rest of the journey. I noticed another man with a slight smile on his face but could not make any accusations with any certainty so, if it was him he got away with it.

On another occasion I was working for a government department, the D.O.E., as a design draftsman. Because of my previous work with a well-known cable manufacturer I was asked to go to Buckingham palace to design some cable routes through rooms that had murals on the walls. This meant the cable had to be hidden as skilfully as possible and what could not be hidden would no doubt have been painted to match the picture behind so they would not be easily detected by any person looking at the picture.

I was studying the wall deep in thought one day when a voice behind me said, "Just what are you supposed to be doing? " Thinking I was alone this startled me and when I turned around there, smiling at me, was Prince Philip. I explained what I was doing and he walked away saying, "Whatever you do, do not spoil any pictures, or steal the silver."

No doubt, this incident was probably not at all memorable for him, but for me the meeting will be remembered for the rest of my life, however long I may live.

When living in Egypt I started working with a man I had met playing snooker. He introduced me to his business partner and friend. Whilst working together I also became friendly with the partner. I cannot say his name for reasons which may become obvious shortly. We all became very good friends, so much so that I was invited to the partners Sister's wedding. At the wedding the bridal couple by tradition sit on a raised dais so that every guest can file up and be introduced and give their congratulations.

However the brides uncle was such a prominent person, who met with the president every day to discuss important matters, that he also sat on a raised dais for people to go up and be introduced to him as well. My friend insisted that I be introduced to his uncle of whom he was very proud. The great man said he knew of me and was very pleased to meet me.

Our friendship had no religious or political elements but was strong nevertheless. It was so strong that when his wedding occurred and I was to be on holiday back in England so could not attend, he changed his plans for his honey moon.

He told his Wife to be that instead of spending three weeks in Italy, which was the original plan, they now were going to spend the first week in England so they could take myself and my Wife to dinner to celebrate the happy event.

With the subsequent events of the ousting of Mubarac and my friends uncle being mentioned in the news at one point as a possible candidate as the new president it appears to be the best policy for me to keep a low profile but I would dearly love to reacquaint myself with this very good friend I think so much of.

At other times of my life I met high profile people. I was introduce to a couple by an old School friend and this led to my meeting many others briefly.

Oxford Street again. I was working for a company and we were involved in the refurbishment of the Mount Royal hotel on Oxford Street. I was walking away from the job after a meeting one day when I was stopped by a small American gentleman. Seeing my briefcase he no doubt thought I would be a good candidate for his pitch.

He talked to me about a company who were selling household products and I became interested. He invited me to a meeting at the Churchill Hotel just round the corner from where we were talking. I agreed to go a couple of nights hence.

When I went to the hotel I recognised the doorman but I had not seen him for a number of years and struggled to remember his name. Suddenly I remembered and said, "Mickey Fields. He said," No I am Brian his Brother, Mick is inside the meeting where you are going, he is working the projector." Needless to say I was very surprised and was eager to remake my acquaintance with them both.

We renewed our friendship and Mick introduced me to a lovely couple called Terry and Sheila Smith. Terry was the road manager of 'Procul Harum' the famous pop group and Sheila had been a singer with a well-known girl group. Terry eventually travelled around the world on tour with Procul about fifteen times. He claimed to be the first pop group manager to be given a company car. It was an Audi 100. Terry and Sheila's son was on his way to being a top session musician. I hope he still is and has carried on using his background to good use, mixing with such phenomenal talent as he did.

Through them I met many pop personalities including Spencer Davis as well as Procul and many other famous people of the day. I well remember the day we went to their house and Spencer Davis's wife Pauline on holiday from America was there with her two boys. The boys had bright green hair because they were blonde and someone had put too much chlorine in their swimming pool.

Eventually Spencer and Pauline divorced and Pauline married Allan from Procul. I have lost touch with them now but I sincerely hope they are all happy and contented with their lot. I have fond memories of them all and will always feel that way.

In nineteen, ninety – three, I was forced by circumstances, to go to work in Saudi Arabia. My work was in Jeddah and I often used to travel to Mecca to work on a power plant there. I carried a letter from the King so, if stopped I could show this and would be allowed to continue even though I was not a Muslim. Being a non -drinker, I used to fill my time by playing ten pin bowling at the local bowling alley. No illegal alcohol for me, thank you very much. At the bowling alley an occasional visitor was one Osama Bin Laden, because the Bin Laden bowling team were in the local league.

The Bin Laden bowling team were always at the bottom of the league. One day, shortly after his family kicked him out and told him they wanted nothing more to do with him, Our bowling team were approached one after the other, by Osama.

One of our team members was a thirteen year old bowling genious who could turn a bowling ball either way with both hands, Junior Ried.

Somehow Osama had got the idea that if he got junior onto his team, they would go to the top of the league and Osama's family would take him back home. Junior's Father also played for our team and we were not about to let such a fine player go, so it never happened.

One day Junior entered an adult competition and I was giving him psychological help, using the principals of Psycho-cybernetics, I had learned from Doctor Maltz. With the maximum score possible being 300 Junior obtained a score of 297 and won the competition.

The first prize being a car, the organisers decide to give Junior the value of the car because he was only thirteen years old.

Junior and his Mother both bought me gold medals with my initials on as my special prize for helping him. Junior bought me a medal with a 'D' printed on it but his Mother bought me two medals, both heart shaped, one with a 'D' and the other with an 'F' and asked me never to tell Junior's Father about it.

Junior's Father was a seventy- two, year old American and his Mother was a forty year old Indonesian with not a single tooth in her head. I never got close to Junior's Mother but I also never said a word to his Father.

Apparently Junior's Father had one year left to go until the end of a very lucrative five year contract and he was determined to retire. Osama had offered him another, five year contract, at twice the salary, but he would not budge one iota. He told us he would have refused even if he was ten years younger, because he would not renege on his contract with us, his buddies.

# The Deceased In My Life

Being a War baby I may have seen many dead people I would not remember. I do remember however, crawling between the legs and over the 'H' bar of a dining chair and, as I emerged I saw my Aunt Dorothy sitting on a bed in front of a Window. My Mother was sitting on one side of her and my Aunt Lily was sitting on the other side. They were trying to comfort My aunt Dorothy who was to die shortly after, at the age of 23 or 24, of Cancer. Aunt Dorothy was crying and the emotion of the whole scene affected me somehow. I crawled across the floor and climbed up the legs of Aunt Dorothy so that I was standing before her. I said, in my childish way. "Don't cry Aunty Dorothy, Suck a sausage." Aunt Dorothy laughed through her tears and cuddled me. My Aunt Lily became my favourite aunt but I feel that, had she lived, it would have been a close thing between her and Aunt Dorothy.

I may have seen some bodies but would have been shielded by my Mother as much as possible and I may have forgotten some things I saw when I was so young. My next memory of seeing a dead body was not quite that.

I was about three or four and we were made to go down into the bomb shelter because of a raid. That night the raid was very heavy and very close to us, so close in fact that we were thrown out of our bunks more than once. When the raid ended it was daylight and everyone had slept very little. A man who must have been in, what was called 'a reserved occupation', said, "Lets go and see what damage has been done." He tried to open the door of the shelter but it stopped after about six inches. He peered around the door and discovered that half a building brick had fallen down the steps leading to the shelter. He was able to remove the obstacle and open the door completely . He climbed the steps, looked to his left and called back, "Well the house is okay, lets go in and make a cup of tea."

He walked round the wall he could see and stopped and swore and said, "Forget that, if the café in the next street is still in one piece we will have to get a cup of tea in there."

When the others went round the wall they discovered that the wall was the only remaining part of the whole terrace that made up the complete side of the street.

If that wall had collapsed it would have buried us and we may not have survived.

Someone then said, "What about the other shelters down the street they must be buried, we must try to find them and get them out, if they are still alive." Someone went to where they thought the nearest shelter was and started scrabbling at the fallen debris.

I, although very small, started to try to help. After a while I saw a hand and called out that I found it. I grabbed it and pulled, and it came out very easily and it was just the hand and part of the arm to just below the elbow. I, in surprise but without any other emotion exclaimed, "Oh". But someone screamed and someone else shouted, "Take it off him."

The hand was grabbed away and I was picked up and cuddled. My next reaction was to wonder at the extreme emotion in the people around me.

Having lived for as long as I have, I have lost many people to death but here I am only telling the stories, mostly, about those I have seen in death.

The first thing I saw does not come strictly into this category but as the person concerned must have ended up dead, from what I knew, I tell this story.

I was only fifteen and illegally in a night club in London, in the middle of the night. The club was seven floors up and had a back door with a small balcony. One day when I had been on the balcony having a smoke break someone I had seen in there before commented on what he called the 'Glory Hole' where I had just carelessly tossed my cigarette butt. He told me the club owner had got into trouble with the shop keepers on the ground floor. They were coming in in the morning and finding this small area, about four or five foot square, formed by sloping corrugated roof's coming close together, full of broken glass and rubbish. Apparently the club patrons were having competitions as to who could get whatever missile they could find through the hole without hitting the sides.

On another occasion, sometime later, I was in the club. Also there and having a good time high on drugs and alcohol were a group of off duty prostitutes. One of their number was continually approaching anyone who was at the Juke box putting on music and requesting they put on a particular song she liked very much. She was making an annoying pest of herself, especially with one man who was at the Juke box many times.

Finally this man got angry and told her where to go in no uncertain terms. The woman had been drinking as well as imbibing whatever drugs she was taking and she in turn got a bit upset and grabbed at his arm when he tried to put his money in the machine.

The man swung his arm away from his body in order to remove her and she became even more upset and started to fight with him.

Her companions seeing what was happening crossed the club and began to join in with gusto. One of them got so carried away that she took off her high heeled shoe and started to hit the man on the head with it. Unfortunately the heel was made of glass with an artificial flower inside. This of course broke which seemed to make her even more angry and she became even more enthusiastic in her attack. The man had become very bloodied by now and seemed to go unconscious. The women kept attacking him for a little longer and then stopped when one of them suggested he might be dead by now.

The other patrons were attempting to leave as quickly as they could. Some had succeeded but others, like myself were trapped by the melee in the middle of the floor. When the fight stopped, those in front of me started to thread their way towards the door. Whilst this was happening the prostitutes, far from being upset, were discussing what they could do with the body. One of them suddenly said "The Glory hole." The people from behind the bar tried to question this and were told nobody would know which flat or office the man had jumped from. This, totally disregarding his injuries from the fight, but left the club staff non-plussed and saying nothing.

The women just picked up the man and carried him to the balcony door, pushing past me as they did so. I hurriedly left the club with the sound of one of the women betting a pound that he would hit the side as he went through.

Although I went back to the club a week or two after, I never heard another thing about the incident. I was too worried about asking anyone because if there was an investigation going on I might get pulled in to it and, because of my age, may have been in more trouble than anyone else. I assumed the man had died but equally possible was that he recovered consciousness and fought his way to his feet and escaped what seemed to be inevitable as I left the premises.

My next brush with death was with my Father. I had a house in Enfield, North London and my Father, Sister and one Brother had moved to the Bournemouth and Poole area. My Father had married my Aunt who, like my Mother was also called Florence, and they lived in a council flat in the area. Unfortunately my Father had become a type two Diabetic as I now have. One day he contracted a common cold and the Doctor gave him some medicine to counteract it. My Father was testing his sugar levels every day and he noticed his sugar level had become too high. He went to his Doctor who should have noted this and never prescribed the medicine in the first place. However the Doctor told my Father to stop taking his medicine, without being specific about which medicine. My Father, not being the brain of Britain, stopped all his medicine including that for his Diabetes. Shortly after this my Father went into a Diabetic coma from which he never recovered.

My Sister informed me he was seriously ill and then two or three days later rang to say he was so bad the Hospital did not think he would last the night. He had been a smoker all his life and this affected him very badly. It was a foggy night but I jumped into my car and drove down to Poole General Hospital travelling at over one hundred miles an hour over the M3 and M27 motorways. I made good time but as I entered the ward he was in, a Nurse was coming out. She asked who I was and on my reply she said "Oh that is so sad, I am just going to inform the Sister. Your Father died a second ago."

She took me in to see him whilst she continued her task of informing the Sister and the two of them came back to speak to me and continue their duty of care towards him.

Whilst I was alone with his body I said goodbye, I hoped he would find peace back with my Mother and Godspeed.

The next person to show me death was an Arab. If as a westerner you work in a strictly Muslim country like Saudi Arabia you will not find too much entertainment of the type you are used to. What happens is that you can purchase and listen to a music machine with radio and whatever mobile music player is dominant on the day, you can go shopping whether of the window or purchasing type or you can find the local illegal alcohol and have a party, at which most people just get drunk, and take a chance on getting arrested.

I personally mostly went shopping and did most of this in the local markets called 'Souks.'

One evening when it was just becoming dark I was in the souk and looking around, I was coming out of one of the gold shops. I was a bit disoriented having seen a man enter the shop with two plastic shopping bags and a cardboard box all full to the brim with paper money. He was greeted by the shop owner who immediately gave him another cardboard box full of paper money and he left the shop with no escort, carrying a box under each arm and a shopping bag in each hand. No doubt he was destined for the bank but he was carrying an absolute fortune in cash, was a small skinny man without any apparent weapon and was just walking in the street without any type of bodyguard or security escort at all.

I felt a little stunned and was not looking properly where I was going. The result of this was I collided with a man walking in the opposite direction. I stumbled back and started to apologise to a man I thought looked like Idi Amin. My face hit his chest, he just smiled and although he was very big he had two escorts both bigger than he was. They were all in army uniform and I am still convinced it was the man but I could not swear to it as I made a hasty exit to get away from his possible wrath.

Thinking I had seen enough for one day I started to walk in the direction of my car. Suddenly I was accosted by a man apparently out of breath who asked if I knew first aid. I said yes and he asked me to follow him. He led me some distance to the side of the road. I asked him where the injured person was. He indicated a cloth lying on the ground with a familiar shape. I lifted the cloth and was presented with a headless body. Feeling shocked I asked him where the head was and he indicated down the road to what, in the gloom of approaching evening, looked like a football in the kerb.

I immediately realised he was not looking for first aid but wanted a foreigner to take the blame for a traffic accident. I ran so fast from the scene that even Usain Bolt would have been left in the dust I kicked up.

The next death I encountered was very sad and upsetting for me.

My Niece had become depressed and I knew nothing about it at first. When I was informed I asked if I could speak to her but my Sister took it on herself to refuse saying she would not wish to speak to me about her problem. I asked again a couple of days later and I was told again she did not want to speak to me and anyway an appointment had been made for her to see the psychiatrist at the local Hospital on the following Tuesday.

I then said to my Sister, "You will be going right past my door so why not bring her in to see me, either before you go to the hospital or after on your way home?"

My Sister said she was too busy and had business appointments booked so she never had time and my niece did not want to speak to me anyway. That night my niece took an overdose of her anti -depression pills and died.

There were several young people who attempted suicide in the area at that time and the media had a ball reporting this.

I made a comment in private linking the whole episode to a TV soap called 'East Enders'.

I deliberately did not make the comment in public but a neighbour who heard me say it, repeated it to the reporters in the hope of being quoted in the media. (Their moment of fame?) Only the comment not the person who said it was reported, I hope they were suitably disappointed.

The cause of my Nieces suicide is down to two things and I feel her depression was not one of them, it was only the thing which led to what happened.

First thing ; *Her Doctor prescribed her a whole month's worth of anti-depression pills and gave them to her to administer to herself.* They should have been given to her Mother to administer in order to prevent her doing what she did, even though she was technically an adult!

Second thing ; *The so called qualified Psychiatrist (who should be struck off) who dismissed her saying she just had a teenage problem which would disappear tomorrow, so she should go away and not bother him.*

NO DEPRESSIVE SHOULD BE DISMISSED AT ANY TIME, IN ANY WAY.

Their condition should be acknowledged and they should be assured that they are not 'alone' and the so called 'qualified practitioner 'would work with them to overcome it. I had given a talk on the Self Image to the staff at that hospital some short time previously and I hope, if I met that doctor at that time, I was not pleasant to them. I consider this person to be a licenced murderer who should be stopped in their tracks .

A Psychiatrist is a medically trained person who may have great knowledge of the brain but has little or no knowledge of the mind.

A psychologist is a person who should have great knowledge of the mind and some knowledge of the brain.

Unfortunately it seems that some Doctors may train minimally on the mind and assume they are now qualified to call themselves Psychiatrist's.

I have no hesitation in condemning an organisation that allows these two acts to be carried out by practitioners. Either act on its own can cause suicide and, putting the two together in this manner will be almost certain to result in this type of tragedy. In fact I would go so far as to say this is 'Iatrogenic Murder'.

I was also very upset with the media who, whilst making the most of the stories about the tragic youngsters who attempted suicide in our local area, allowed my Sister, in her very upset state of mind because of her tragic loss, to appear on television to make a statement.

Instead of checking and editing her statement they just put it out in its untouched entirety. She tried defending my niece by saying her daughter was not of unsound mind but did what she intended doing as if it were the act of a normal person with high intellect and in a perfectly logical manner.

To me this did not show my Sister in a good light and must surely have made some people wonder about her. I know I heard some people refer to the broadcast in a doubtful state of mind.

After the event I had two persons come to me for counselling and they both made comments about it. One person was the ex- boyfriend of my niece who was implicated badly in her act. He was totally innocent and just a young man doing what young people do and had ended their relationship just the same as any young person may have done.

Although this act could be said to have had a bad reaction in my Niece, the act of maintaining their relationship could have been bad for both their future's anyway. I hope from our conversations he went away not too badly affected by the whole affair and able to go from that place and have as normal a life as was possible.

The other person who came to see me for counselling was a woman who knew one of the other young persons who was successful in committing suicide at that time. This young lady was trying to get back her boyfriend after an argument that she thought had ended their relationship. She took an overdose of Paracetamol and after twelve hours told her boyfriend what she had done.

She was rushed to hospital and her stomach pumped but unfortunately it was too late.

The lady I was counselling had seen her on the following day after her stomach was pumped. She said she was sitting up in her hospital bed, her boyfriend was back in her life and she was looking beautiful and healthy and full of life. Unfortunately the paracetamol had done its work and killed an essential enzyme in her stomach and the very next day she died, looking very healthy but not being so.

Approximately two years later a man came to see me who had been diagnosed as schizophrenic. He felt that I had helped him to cope with his condition and we were both snooker players and met by chance subsequent to our sessions together. We ended up becoming friends, we liked each other and I was interested in how his condition affected him on a day to day basis.

One day we had been playing snooker together and were sitting outside my front gate late at night and just talking generally. Suddenly he said, "The voices in my head are talking to me and saying they have a message for you." He went on to describe two people whom he could not possibly know who had been in my life previously.

He said I am being told to tell you that Lisa Is fine, she is with Rose who is looking after her and they are both very happy. He described them both very accurately and the strangest thing about this was that he described Rose as wearing a housemaids uniform, she had worked as a maid more than twenty years before I met her. I only knew this because her Husband refused to let her work when she wanted to later in life and the subject of her previous work had come up.

The voices in his head were apparently getting worse and one day Tony did something he had never done in his life before, he asked someone, me, to drive his car because the voices in his head were trying to persuade him to drive into on- coming traffic. We were on a trip to Bath with some friends in the car and he was very worried that he could not refuse the voices demand's.

As a result of this he said that only I could drive his car and when he died I was to have his car for myself. I ignored this as I thought he would have a very different car by the time he eventually died.

However death must have already been on his mind and a few months later Tony hung himself through the trapdoor to the roof space in his house, with the rope tied to the roof beams above. I did not get his car because his Sister sold it very cheaply to a so called friend who knew of Tony's intent but ignored it because the car came so cheaply to her. I ended up having to pay five pounds each to buy Tony's golf clubs as something to remember him by.

I have known many others who have died, some tragically and some who have caused me a great deal of emotional upset. I think that maybe I was somewhat lucky not to have seen all of them in death but that does not diminish their passing in any way.

Printed in the United States
by Baker & Taylor Publisher Services